ACTUALITY OF BEING

Dzogchen and Tantric Perspectives

Books by Traleg Kyabgon

Vajrayana: An Essential Guide to Practice, Shogam Publications, 2020

Desire: Why It Matters, Shogam Publications, 2019

Integral Buddhism: Developing All Aspects of One's Personhood, Shogam Publications, 2018

King Doha: Saraha's Advice to a King, Shogam Publications, 2018

Letter to a Friend: Nagarjuna's Classic Text, Shogam Publications, 2018

Song of Karmapa: The Aspiration of the Mahamudra of True Meaning by Lord Rangjung Dorje, Shogam Publications, 2018

Moonbeams of Mahamudra: The Classic Meditation Manual, Shogam Publications, 2015

Karma: What it is, What it isn't, and Why it matters, Shambhala Publications, 2015

Four Dharmas of Gampopa, KTD Publications, 2013

Asanga's Abhidharmasamuccaya, KTD Publications, 2013

Ninth Karmapa Wangchuk Dorje's Ocean Of Certainty, KTD Publications, 2011

Influence of Yogacara on Mahamudra, KTD Publications, 2010

The Practice of Lojong: Cultivating Compassion through Training the Mind, Shambhala Publications, 2007

Mind at Ease: Self-Liberation through Mahamudra Meditation, Shambhala Publications, 2004

Benevolent Mind: A Manual in Mind Training, Zhyisil Chokyi Ghatsal Publications, 2003

Photo facing page: Traleg Kyabgon Rinpoche the Ninth

ACTUALITY OF BEING
Dzogchen and Tantric Perspectives

Traleg Kyabgon

Foreword by Dzigar Kongtrül Rinpoche

SHOGAM
PUBLICATIONS
2020

Shogam Publications Pty Ltd
PO Box 239 Ballarat Central
Victoria, Australia, 3353
www.shogam.org
info@shogam.com

Printed in Australia and the United States of America

Edited and Designed by David Bennett
Library Reference
Kyabgon, Traleg, 1955
Actuality of Being: Dzogchen and Tantric Perspectives

Printed book ISBN: 978-0-6483321-7-6 (Paperback)
E-book ISBN: 978-0-6483321-8-3

DEDICATION

To the great lineage holders of intrinsic awareness who have continuously transmitted the teachings, and in particular to Traleg Kyabgon Rinpoche IX who worked tirelessly to present these teachings in the west.

Contents

Foreword

The Dzogpa Chenpo teachings are the summit of the nine yanas. A vajra master of the highest category like Guru Padmasambhava, along with many others of the Nyingma and Kagyu lineages, can transfer or point out the state of the great perfection in a flash of their enlightened blessings. This state is known as rigpa changchup kyi sem. The great Dzogchen master Rongdzom Chudrak stated, the difference between sentient beings and enlightened ones is only a thin veil. That veil is drawn between having recognition of the state of rigpa or not. And in *Samantabhadra's Aspiration* it similarly states, sentient beings and enlightened ones arise from the same source; upon recognition of the state of rigpa Samantabhadra came to be the primordial Buddha, while sentient beings, due to their lack of recognition came to be themselves. In either case, the nature has never gone anywhere. When the sun goes behind a cloud it does not seem to shine, yet the sun is ever present in the sky. The teachings of the Dzogpa Chenpo can reveal one's own ever present enlightened nature if one has the merit to make a connection to a Dzogpa Chenpo master and the teachings.

Traleg Kyabgon Rinpoche is a great master of our time particularly for the western audience. He has lived much of his life for the benefit of his western students and his deeds and compassion are themselves proof of his great mastery of Dzogpa Chenpo and Mahamudra. This book is a great inspiration and deeply illuminating for those seriously pursuing this path. In studying this text may we all appreciate, enjoy, and remember his presence with us.

Dzigar Kongtrül Rinpoche

Biography of Author
TRALEG KYABGON RINPOCHE IX

Traleg Kyabgon Rinpoche IX (1955-2012) was born in Nangchen in Kham, eastern Tibet. He was recognized by His Holiness XVI Gyalwang Karmapa as the ninth Traleg tulku and enthroned at the age of two as the supreme abbot of Thrangu Monastery. Rinpoche was taken to Rumtek Monastery in Sikkim at the age of four where he was educated with other young tulkus in exile by His Holiness Karmapa for the next five years.

Rinpoche began his studies under the auspices of His Eminence Kyabje Thuksey Rinpoche at Sangngak Choling in Darjeeling. He also studied with a number of other eminent Tibetan teachers during that time and mastered the many Tibetan teachings with the Kagyu and Nyingma traditions in particular, including the *Havajra Tantra, Guhyasamaja Tantra*, and the third Karmapa's *Zabmo Nangdon (The Profound Inner Meaning)* under Khenpo Noryang (abbot of Sangngak Choling). Rinpoche studied the *Abhidharmakosha, Pramanavarttika, Bodhisattvacharyavatara, Abhidharmasamuccaya, Six Treaties of Nagarjuna*, the *Madhyanta-vibhaga*, and the *Mahayanuttaratantra* with Khenpo Sogyal. He also studied with Khenpo Sodar and was trained in tantric ritual practices by Lama Ganga, who had been specifically sent by His Holiness Karmapa for that purpose.

In 1967 Rinpoche moved to the Institute of Higher Tibetan Studies in Sarnath, and studied extensively for the next five years. He studied Buddhist history, Sanskrit, and Hindi, as well as Longchenpa's *Finding Comfort and Ease (Ngalso Korsum), Seven Treasuries (Longchen Dzod Dun), Three Cycles of Liberation (Rangdrol Korsum)*, and *Longchen Nyingthig* with Khenchen Palden Sherab Rinpoche and Khenpo Tsondru.

When Rinpoche had completed these studies at the age of sixteen, he was sent by His Holiness Karmapa to study under the auspices of the Venerable Khenpo Yesha Chodar at Sanskrit University in Varanasi for three years. Rinpoche was also tutored by khenpos and geshes from all four traditions of Tibetan Buddhism during this time.

Rinpoche was subsequently put in charge of Zangdog Palri Monastery (the glorious copper colored mountain) in Eastern Bhutan and placed under the private tutelage of Dregung Khenpo Ngedon by His Holiness Karmapa to continue his studies of Sutra and Tantra. He ran this monastery for the next three years and began learning English during this time.

From 1977 to 1980, Rinpoche returned to Rumtek in Sikkim to fill the honored position of His Holiness' translator, where he dealt with many English-speaking Western visitors.

Rinpoche moved to Melbourne, Australia in 1980 and commenced studies in comparative religion and philosophy at LaTrobe University. Rinpoche established E-Vam Institute in Melbourne in 1982 and went on to establish further Centers in Australia, America, and New Zealand. For the next 25 years Rinpoche gave weekly teachings, intensive weekend courses, and retreats on classic Kagyu and Nyingma texts. During this time Rinpoche also taught internationally travelling extensively through America, Europe, and South East Asia and was appointed the Spiritual Director of Kamalashila Institute in Germany for five years in the 1980's.

Rinpoche established a retreat center, Maitripa Centre in Healesville, Australia in 1997 where he conducted two public retreats a year. Rinpoche founded E-Vam Buddhist Institute in the U.S in 2000, and Nyima Tashi Buddhist Centre in New Zealand in 2004. In 2010 Rinpoche established a Buddhist college called Shogam Vidhalaya at E-Vam Institute in Australia and instructed students on a weekly basis.

Throughout his life Rinpoche gave extensive teachings on many aspects of Buddhist psychology and philosophy, as well as comparative religion, and Buddhist and Western thought. He was an active writer and has many titles to his name. Titles include: the best selling *Essence of Buddhism; Desire: Why It Matters; Vajrayana: An Essential Guide to Practice; Moonbeams of Mahamudra; Karma What It Is, What It Isn't, and Why It Matters; The Practice of Lojong;* and many more. Many of Rinpoche's books are translated into a number of different languages including Chinese, French, German, Korean, and Spanish. Rinpoche's writings are thought provoking, challenging, profound, and highly relevant to today's world and its many challenges.

Rinpoche was active in publishing during the last two decades of his life, beginning with his quarterly magazine *Ordinary Mind,* which ran from 1997 to 2003. Further, Rinpoche founded his own publishing arm Shogam Publications in 2008 and released a number of books on Buddhist history, philosophy, and psychology and left instructions for the continuation of this vision. His vision for Shogam and list of titles can be found at www.shogam.com.

Rinpoche's ecumenical approach can be seen in his other activities aimed at bringing buddhadharma to the West. He established the biannual Buddhism and Psychotherapy Conference (1994 - 2003), and Tibet Here and Now Conference (2005), and the annual Buddhist Summer School (1984 to the present).

Traleg Kyabgon Rinpoche IX passed into parinirvana on 24 July 2012, on Chokhor Duchen, the auspicious day of the Buddha's first teaching. Rinpoche stayed in meditation (*thugdam*) for weeks after his passing. A traditional cremation ceremony was conducted at Maitripa Centre and a stupa was erected on the center's grounds in Rinpoche's honor.

It is a privilege to continue Rinpoche's vision and initiatives, and to continue to make the profound teachings of Traleg Kyabgon Rinpoche IX given in the West for over 30 years available through his Centers' activities and Shogam Publications. Rinpoche's Sangha hope that many will benefit.

Acknowledgements

Thanks to everyone at Shogam for their tireless efforts and ongoing contributions to making Traleg Rinpoche's vast array of teachings available. In particular to Salvatore Celiento for his keen eye for detail and meticulous proofing; to Traleg Khandro for her editorial support and unceasing commitment and activity; and to Jampa Dhadrak La for his expertise on the Tibetan and Sanskrit terms and for composing the glossary.

Finally, I would especially like to thank Dzogchen Ponlop Rinpoche for his kind permission to include the history of the Dzogchen lineage in the editor's introduction taken from teachings he presented on Dzogchen at E-Vam Institute in Melbourne, Australia.

David Bennett

Editor's Introduction

Although Dzogchen, or Maha Ati, is generally presented within the nine yana system of the Nyingma tradition of Tibetan Buddhism, it exists independently of any system and is not considered a school of thought as such, within or outside of Buddhism. A complete path in itself, Dzogchen emphasizes the notion of sudden or instantaneous enlightenment, or self-liberation, and that whether we know it or not, we have always existed in our authentic condition. As Traleg Rinpoche states, "In Dzogchen practice the beginning and the end are not separate. The very starting point is the end itself. There is no difference between the alpha and omega, in the sense that when you realize Dzogchen, you have not realized anything different from what you already possess."

Compiled from a series of Dzogchen retreats conducted by Traleg Kyabgon Rinpoche, *Actuality of Being: Dzogchen and Tantric Perspectives* takes us on a remarkable journey, bringing the profundity and subtleties of Dzogchen to life in a way that makes approaching this advanced, but essentially simple path achievable. Rinpoche encourages a flexibility of mind throughout this book, and points out the important distinctions between religiosity and spirituality, and morality and ethics. He clarifies the nine yana system and the tantric approach in relation to Dzogchen, and elaborates on key aspects of the view, meditation, and action of Dzogchen practice. By developing a more open attitude, and by coming in touch with our authentic condition, Rinpoche suggests it is possible to relate directly with ourselves and the world fully, and be responsive to the causes and conditions that manifest at any given time. Along with his comprehensive presentation of the Dzogchen teachings, Rinpoche gives several simple yet profound practice methods to deepen one's understanding and experience.

Lineage

The notion of lineage is very important in Dzogchen. There are three aspects of lineage—three fundamental transmissions, or three fundamental states of awakening called "the three lineages."

The first lineage is "the thought lineage of the victorious ones," the victorious ones being the Buddhas. It is also known as "the intentional lineage of Buddha," or "the thought lineage." "Thought" here doesn't mean concept, it means essence, space, the fundamental space of Dzogchen. It is actually pre-thought, something at the very beginning, or primordial. It is the basic primordial space, which is extraordinarily wide and open space.

This lineage is the basic lineage of the three kayas which is taking place in primordial space, timelessly. That is symbolized by Samantabhadra Buddha, the primordial Buddha or Dharmakaya Buddha, who is depicted as blue and naked. The lineage of the Dharmakaya Buddha is ever-present in primordial space. It never started at a given point in time, it is never ceasing, it never existed, it is ever-present, and the transmission of the primordial Buddha, Samantabhadra Buddha, is continuous in every moment of space.

The Dharmakaya Buddha manifests in the Samabhogakaya as Vajradhara Buddha. Vajradhara is depicted as blue in color holding a bell and dorje across his heart. The Sambhogakaya Buddha is not separate from the Samantabhara Buddha, it is the luminous or clarity aspect of Samantabhadra. Vajradhara self-emanates light and continues the teaching, continues the thought lineage, or the intentional lineage of the Buddhas, without words into the realm of *akanishtha*, the pure realm of the Sambhogakaya Buddhas.

The Nirmanakaya Buddha then manifests as the five Buddha

families and continues the thought lineage of the primordial Buddha through the five different activities of the Buddha—Vairocana Buddha, Akshobya Buddha, Ratnasambhava Buddha, Amitabha Buddha, and Amogasiddi Buddha.

The second lineage is "the symbolic lineage of the Vidyadharas." Vidyadhara means "holder of the rigpa transmission," "holder of bare awareness." This lineage is also known as "the symbolic lineage of the yogis," or "the sign lineage."

This is the lineage where one sees every aspect of the phenomenal world as recognition of rigpa. Every aspect of the phenomenal world is a symbol that gives one the awakening experience of a primordial Buddha. At this stage there is a certain sense of development into a traditional lineage where great masters, yogis, and Buddhas in the past, have carried on this symbolic lineage. Everything is taught and understood through simple sign, simple symbol. At the stage of the symbolic lineage communication is as simple as Ah. The whole communication, the whole teachings, the whole understanding, and the realization, is a product of Ah.

The third lineage is called "the ear whispered lineage," or "oral lineage of mundane individuals." This is the living lineage of the Dzogchen tradition, which is passed down from one master to another. It is coming down more to the nirmanakaya Buddha level where all levels of beings can talk and communicate.

The first human master of Dzogchen was Garab Dorje who was from the kingdom of Uddiyana in northern India. Vajrasattva appeared to Garab Dorje, empowered him and instructed him to write down the Dzogchen Tantras. The transmission then passed to Manjushrimitra, Shri Singha, and Jnanasutra through the the symbolic lineage of the Vidyadharas. Sri Singha transmitted it to Padmasambhava who brought this lineage to Tibet some time in the late seventh or early eighth century. From Padmasambhava onwards is counted as the ear whispered lineage which remains unbroken and continues to the present day.

Two aspects of lineage

The Dzogchen lineage has been kept alive through two aspects, the karma lineage and the terma lineage. Karma lineage refers to the ear whispered lineage, or oral lineage of mundane individuals, that has been passed down from teacher to student.

The terma lineage refers to teachings that have been rediscovered. Terma literally means "rediscovery," or "rediscovered." Termas are teachings that have already been discovered by such masters as Sri Singha, Padmasambhava, and Jnanasutra, and have then been buried or hidden by Padmasambhava. He buried or hid certain Dzogchen teachings to be rediscovered in later centuries to benefit beings. Those teachings were buried or hidden in different forms, different places. There are earth terma, sky terma, water terma, and space or thought terma, and those terma teachings have been rediscovered by the heart sons and daughters of Padmasambhava in later times and propagated, expanded, and taught extensively in different forms.

Three cycles of Dzogchen

Dzogchen is presented through three cycles, or series: semde, longde, and mennagde. These are three different ways of presenting the teachings with corresponding methods of practice.

Semde is the "mind series," and emphasizes the recognition of the true essence of mind and of phenomenal appearance, and the inseparability of awareness and appearance in the essence of rigpa, or self-existing wisdom.

Longde is the "inner space series," and refers to the primordial dimension of space, the inner space of a primordial Buddha, where everything arises as wisdom. Longde practice is unfabricated and emphasizes freedom of effort. It is known as having unmistaken view, the view that is free from any deception.

Mennagde is the "essential series of secret instructions," comprised of teachings and methods based on the experiences of past masters. The core of the Mennagde are the Nyingtik or "Heart Essence" teachings.

Two paths

Dzogchen incorporates two paths, or methods: Trekcho and Thogal.

Trekcho means "cutting through," and reveals the view of primordial purity beyond conceptual elaboration through combining intrinsic awareness and emptiness. When the clarity of rigpa is revealed, all of our samsaric views and beliefs are destroyed or cut through.

Thogal means "leaping over," and is related with the integration of appearance and emptiness. It works directly with the internal and external luminosity by employing certain postures and gazes. Thogal practice can only be undertaken once a practitioner has gained stability in the practice of Trekcho.

Although one may study and practice the Dzogchen teachings presented in this book, misunderstandings of both the teachings, and experiences that one may undergo in the process of meditation can easily occur, and one may go astray. For this reason, it is necessary to study and practice under the guidance of an authentic Dzogchen master in order to clarify any confusions one may have in order to develop on the path.

The world we live in is undergoing dramatic changes and we are confronted with difficult conditions and an uncertain future. Though much of what takes place in the world may not be within our control, by studying and practicing the Dzogchen teachings we may experience a greater sense of freedom and ease, regardless of the ever-changing events taking place in the phenomenal world.

David Bennett

ACTUALITY OF BEING

Dzogchen and Tantric Perspectives

Chapter One

Religion, Spirituality, and Self-Knowledge

When we talk about religion and spirituality, we do not normally make sharp distinctions between the two. Somehow these two concepts get conflated. Even though these two ideas are intimately related they can also be seen as distinctive. From the point of view of religion, there is a connection with certain sacred texts, rituals, and so on. For instance, at birth, the child may be initiated into a particular religious order. They may have a birth ceremony, and there may be all kinds of significant ceremonies along the way, until the final death ceremony. However, religion does not necessarily deal with an individual's life particularly. One may have strong religious convictions and one may have strong emotional attitudes involved with some particular religious belief systems, but nonetheless, the whole process can remain quite impersonal.

If we look at spirituality, it can be seen quite differently. When a person develops a spiritual approach, they can become liberated from certain religious constrictions that are placed on them. They may stop being reliant on religious authority, rituals, and holy texts and begin to turn within. Instead of living day by day, and living life by the book, one begins to question one's attitude towards religious practice, and can start to question the values of certain religious convictions that have been held. One begins to become more spontaneous, open-minded, and less dogmatic. One can be a religious person and be dogmatic, but if one becomes a spiritual person, then one is instigating a process towards being totally undogmatic.

We can see that by becoming spiritual, one is also beginning to enquire into the possibilities of building self-knowledge. What is meant by self-knowledge? If we start to look into that, we realize that self-knowledge has to do with the understanding of our self, and that is not all. Self-knowledge also has to do with our understanding of others. Usually, when we talk about self-knowledge, we tend to think that self-knowledge requires us to dig deeper and deeper into ourselves to begin to know something about ourselves. However, if we do not include others, the more we dig into ourselves, the more we are likely to find nothing but confusion and a disarrayed state of being. It is sometimes much easier to look at someone and see what they are going through, what their attitude is, how they are managing things, and how they conduct their life, than to look at ourselves.

We can look at another person in an involved way, without being overwhelmed. However, when we become too self-engrossed, no matter how much we try to discover things about ourselves and our situation, it can become more and more overwhelming. In this particular context, when we start to look at self-knowledge, we need to remember that knowing oneself is developed in conjunction with understanding and knowing more about the human condition, and thus knowing others.

When we look at other people, we are usually completely governed by concepts and labels. Buddhism talks about the limitations of concepts and labels, and the importance of seeing their limitations in a very personal way. Even though we may understand these limitations, the strong habitual tendency is to continue to use them. If we begin to look at the limitations of concepts and labels, we can realize that generalizations are the worst enemies towards self-understanding and self-knowledge.

We have an inveterate tendency to label people. We always categorize people in different ways so we have a neat system that gives us something quite definite. For example, we may believe a particular person is very aggressive or lazy, and so on. If we deal with people in that way, then we do not understand a person at all. Rather, what we understand is the image that we have created of that particular person because no one is just a totally aggressive person or a totally lazy person. Therefore, when we are dealing with individuals, it is extremely important to look at the person's individual circumstances and situations. A person is never made up of just one thing; a person is made up of an amalgamation of things, which Buddhists call the "five skandhas." The five skandhas, also known as the "five aggregates," or "five heaps," are an amalgamation of a variety of characteristics that challenge the idea that any person can be categorized by putting a label on them.

The five skandhas are: 1. Form—your physical body. Traditionally, these are listed as the eyes, ears, nose, tongue, and body and mind. 2. Feeling—the sensations you experience in your body, including all pain and pleasure. 3. Perception—the sense organs, and the corresponding sense objects. Put them together— eye and light, nose and smell, et cetera, and you have perception. 4. Mental formations—all your concepts and thoughts, from the most mundane to the most sublime. 5. Consciousness—your awareness of the first four skandhas, form through to perception.

Along with overcoming excessive categorization is the importance of overcoming duality. That is, looking at religious and metaphysical concepts much more personally. Usually we have all kinds of dualistic metaphysical and religious concepts such as god, the world, the self, eternity and temporality, being and becoming, and so on. What we develop is a world completely constructed in our own head, which is totally polarizing. On one side we have good, eternity, being, and on the other side, we have becoming, temporality, and suffering. We are going to look at those polarized concepts and look at the possibility of overcoming such a dualistic predicament that we have personally established. We are going to be looking at how to transcend the particular predicament of duality.

People often wish to be a part of a religion due to a personal feeling of temporality and a broad sense of uncertainty. The metaphysical concepts of being, god, eternity, and so forth, are used as a form of security, so that while we are still subjected to change, there is an underlying belief that there is something beyond the uncertainty that does not change, that is totally beautiful and perfect.

In the context of this book, we won't be looking at *Dzogchen* from a religious perspective as much as looking at the possibilities of transcendence, transcendence from dualistic concepts such as being and becoming, eternity and temporality, self and world, and so on. According to Dzogchen, the world we live in is subject to changes, becoming, and temporality. These are not qualities or experiences that one needs to escape from or discard. Rather, it addresses the idea of being fully involved and fully engaged, which is not something we normally manage to do. Instead of assuming that the life we are leading, or the world that we live in is dissatisfactory or evil, we need to be more directly in touch with the world without the overlay or separation created by presumption and predetermined beliefs.

The Dzogchen system of teachings does not give any way out of this particular sort of experience of the world. It describes how we can better relate to the world that we live in. It is also involved with life-enhancement and trying to understand the present situation much better and overcome the resentment against time. In our minds, temporality can be seen as a most evil thing.

We can feel completely helpless knowing that we cannot undo

something we wish we had not done, or do what we had failed to do. Because we know we cannot change the past, we can feel completely helpless or even resentment against time. Also, we may embark on particular projects or behaviors to bring about certain predetermined results, building a type of future with great expectations. When our expectations are not achieved or the circumstances do not arise as we had hoped, resentment against time can arise again, and the impending death that we all experience can be seen as the ultimate resentment against time.

Understanding temporality and working to overcome resentment and helplessness against temporality is at the foundation of Dzogchen practice. Understanding this pervasive condition can help us develop an ability to face uncertainty more courageously, thus curbing our seemingly innate tendency to flee such pervasive uncertainty by constructing all kinds of mental concepts of eternity and certainty.

From the Dzogchen point of view, the other Buddhist schools of thought such as Hinayana, Mahayana, and Vajrayana or Tantra, are seen as providing different approaches and perspectives to addressing the samsaric condition. Hinayana is seen as the approach of renunciation; Mahayana as the approach of purification; and Vajrayana or Tantra as that of transformation or transmutation.

Dzogchen practice is known as the approach of self-liberation. In this approach, the practitioner is not trying to transmute or transform themselves into something sublime or elevated, as is the case in Tantra. Rather, the approach directly confronts what arises in the mind, whatever presents itself. Whatever one experiences is seen as it is, free of extrapolation. Whatever problem one may have thought existed in the past can be seen freshly as it arises, and ceases to present itself as a problem. The problem begins to get resolved on the spot. This is why it is known as the path of self-liberation.

The notion of self-liberation has developed because in the

Dzogchen tradition there is not a set view. Dzogchen practitioners do not hold a particular philosophical view, unlike most other schools. The Dzogchen tradition considers all Buddhist schools of thought, and the varieties of views within those schools and those of other religious traditions, are simply seen as different views based upon different value systems. Therefore, all the views are seen as relative. There is no absolute view as there is no absolute knowledge. Such a conclusion is drawn from looking into our experience of the world. We can find we do not experience anything that is eternal or has eternal essence. We observe the process of change and flux, the juxtaposition of varieties of forces, different causes and conditions interacting, coming into and out of existence.

When we begin to investigate the temporality of our situation, what we have seen or what we have known is recognized as relative. Our experience of what we have seen and known in the past has become extinct, and something new has replaced it. Even if we look at something that seems to be fairly stable and persistent in time, that seeming persistence of an experience or object turns out to not be persistent. There is absolutely nothing that has not gone through changes, no matter how gradual the changes happen to be.

By recognizing the temporality of the world and our experience, the concept of identity, of thing-hood, of person-hood, and the concept of the agent and action, is thrown into chaos. We usually think that a person has an identity—that the person who was born on a certain day, in a certain year, is the same as the person who is living now. However, the person is still the same person, but at the same time they are not same, because they have completely changed over time. We acknowledge that we have changed physically, but mentally, we may believe there is something inside of us that is totally solid, unlike a material object—therefore it must persist. If one believes in reincarnation, one can have the view that something unchanging has been there before we are born, and will persist after we die. Even then, in relation to consciousness, nothing is seen as unchanging.

When we start to think about how we make this division between mind and body, the concept of our experience, concept of objects, and concept of a stable world, et cetera, we begin to realize that all this is based upon interpretation. It is a conceptual construction which does not correspond to the reality of things at all.

When we start to develop this kind of attitude, we begin to realize that any kind of view that we might cultivate can only be relative. Also, any kind of knowledge that we might accumulate can only be relative, as knowledge of anything unchanging and persistent without the potential for extinction cannot be found. Whatever we experience, whatever we know of, is relational, and therefore completely relative. Therefore, if what we know and experience is relative, then the knowledge itself must be relative as well. We can't know of something that is relative and then feel that the knowledge is something eternal and immutable. Therefore, it is said that in Dzogchen, the only view that one can develop is what we might call perspectivism—all views and attitudes are only a perspective we hold in relation to a particular thing, experience, or event.

This kind of attitude does not lead to nihilism, as some might think. Relativism can be frightening because if everything is seen as fundamentally based on perspective, fixed notions such as good and evil are also seen as temporal, which can put into question the idea of a fixed moral structure. Concerns of a moral structure being undermined can arise. Will we revert back to barbarism? Rather, relativism gives us the opportunity to have a different perspective on morality. Moral belief systems are often grounded in religious and metaphysical views where human beings are seen as amoral by nature, and therefore, morality has given the gift of standards and certainty in how to behave, which is often seen as extraordinarily precious. However, in this context, morality is not defined in terms of abiding by rules, regulations, and what one ought to do, but rather based more on the person's honesty. A person's honesty comes about by realizing that one no longer needs to deceive oneself by pretending to be moral or wishing to be seen as moral. Rather than abiding by certain rules and regulations set out by others, one tends to take fuller responsibility oneself. When we abide by rules and regulations that are preset, it may be easier to be moral, but that may make it extremely difficult to be honest.

There are a lot of notions, even in Buddhism, whereby the whole idea of morality is based on reward and punishment, so we become like the Pavlovian dog[1]—if we do certain things we will be rewarded, other behaviors and attitudes will be punished. We don't become moral because we have decided that is the best course of action to take, but rather, we become moral out of fear, because we don't want to be punished. It can be argued that society's structure is based on that model and it is instilled in us from childhood on.

In the Dzogchen teachings, there are no strict rules as such, mainly because good and evil are not seen as independent and permanent. Rather than being seen as a fixed aspect or feature of the world, they are seen as part of one's own psychological state of mind. Good and evil are not seen as eternal principles, but rather are seen as being subject to time, based upon historical and temporal events, so therefore they are not seen as absolute.

Instead of leading to nihilism where all values are thrown away, it gives us a real meaning in life. It provides the opportunity to connect to life. Instead of trying to escape, we can go back to our true condition that has always been there. The meaning of life is found within life itself. What we normally do is try to find the meaning of life from outside. To do this, we often adhere to immutable principles and concepts such as god, because of our need to have a meaningful existence. In this particular case, meaning and fulfilment is found within the mutable, so the process is reversed.

The meaning of life cannot be found by constructing all kinds of metaphysical and transcendental concepts, but rather by trying to become more in touch with our own existence, by coming in touch with who we are. We may say, "I want to find out who I am, what I am." This suggests we are looking for something we have never found or experienced before, which can lead to the development of all kinds of concepts like immutable soul, divine spark, and so on. However, striving to find out "who I am" is based on the concept of "who I am now." "Who I am now" is arrived at through trying to ignore certain aspects of ourselves and cultivate other aspects of ourselves, and we haven't really got any particular idea about who we actually are.

In the Dzogchen context, the discovery of who we are relates to becoming more in touch with ourselves. This is not done in order to pull away the layers and layers of obscurations veiling our true nature, but rather to try to see ourselves in a different way than what we normally do. When people say there are unconscious processes that we don't know about, it need not be seen as if the unconscious is hidden underneath and the consciousness is on the surface. It is a metaphor, it does not mean that unconsciousness is literally underneath the consciousness. Even when we say, "Our true nature," it does not mean that our true nature is somehow hidden inside our heart. Fundamentally, what it means is to be able to have a holistic view of ourselves. This means to unreservedly see our good and bad aspects, to develop a uniform idea of who we are.

Chapter Two

The Nine Yana System

Before we go through what is referred to as the "Nine Yana System" within the Nyingma tradition, we need to look at what is meant by "*dharma*." Buddhism is a translation of the Sanskrit word dharma, *cho* in Tibetan.

There are many meanings associated with the word dharma. It can be very confusing because it has been used in varieties of contexts with different connotations and denotations. This is just a summary of the number of ways in which it can be used: to differentiate what is proper and what is improper—a dharmic way of doing something, or a non-dharmic way of doing something—in that sense, one uses it in an evaluative manner; it can be used in order to denote scriptures; at other times the word dharma is used in order to denote social customs; it is used in the sense of secular law or the custom of a particular country or nation; and it is used in order to denote both material and psychological entities.

When the word dharma is used in the context of this book, it is used in conjunction with the last two noble truths, the truth of the path and the truth of cessation. What is meant by this is that the word dharma, in this particular context, has to do with overcoming and eradicating our defilements and being able to cultivate necessary spiritual qualities to become enlightened. Both of these—overcoming defilements and cultivating spiritual qualities—are intimately related with the last two truths.

When the word dharma is used in this sense, then it assumes two aspects. The first aspect is called "understanding," *thogpa* in Tibetan, and is also referred to as "the subject of discourse," *jod ja* in Tibetan. The second is "exposition," which is called *lung* in Tibetan, the method of discourse.

Understanding has three characteristics: ineffability, non-divisiveness, and devoid of subject and object.

In this context "ineffability" means that when the understanding emerges, it does not arise as an idea, as something that we conceptually think about, but it dawns in the practitioner in a non-discursive manner. It is called *jod du med pa* in Tibetan, which means inconceivable. Because it is inconceivable, it is therefore ineffable.

"Non-divisiveness" refers to the emergence of understanding, as it manifests in the practitioner. Then there are no mental conflicts—therefore the person is at peace, *zhiwa* in Tibetan. So non-divisiveness leads to the experience of peace.

"Devoid of subject and object" means that when the understanding emerges, then the person is no longer disposed to a rational understanding of things, *thogpa me pa* in Tibetan.

"Understanding" has nothing to do with philosophies, schools of thought, or viewpoints. When discussing Dzogchen, we will discover that it relates to pure experience, it does not have any viewpoints as such. However, in terms of exposition, in terms of method of discourse, which is the second aspect, then one tries to use concepts and ideas, because it is through the method of discourse that one can have some understanding. We can then conceptually align with the subject of discourse, jod ja.

The method of discourse, the exposition, has three aspects. The first aspect is the subject matter. The subject matter of the method of discourse is called *lab pa sum* in Tibetan, "the three trainings." These are: training in morality, *tsultrim kyi lab pa* in Tibetan; training in meditation, *ting nge zin gi lab pa* in Tibetan; and training in transcendental knowledge, *sherab ki lab pa* in Tibetan.

The second aspect is the discourse conducted in a completely unsullied manner. All the words and sentences that are being used are not tainted by emotional afflictions, conceptual confusions, nor do the words and sentences generate conceptual confusions and emotional conflicts.

The third aspect refers to the method, or how the exposition is conducted. It is conducted in three different ways. Firstly, through direct sense perception, secondly, through inference, and thirdly, through citation of authoritative texts.

In brief, as the *Uttaratantra*[2] says, the exposition is conducted in such a manner that it is meaningful and that it is able to eradicate the emotional conflicts of all sentient beings, and finally that it is able to advance the view of the benefit of attaining nirvana. Therefore, all these should be taken as the teachings of the Buddha and all expositions that oppose it should be recognized as not being Buddhist teachings.

As previously stated, the subject of the exposition are the three trainings. Corresponding to those three trainings are what are known as the "three baskets," or *tripitaka*. These consist of the teachings on the *vinaya*, *sutra*, and *abhidharma*. The teachings of the vinaya, *dulwa* in Tibetan, are the moral discourses. The moral discourses are given in order to improve our moral standard. It is said that we yield to our temptations and we fall short of moral standards basically through three factors. The first one is lack of mindfulness, the second is excess in emotional conflicts, and the third one is lack of humility. In order to improve our mind and meditation, then the sutra teachings are given. In order to increase our transcendental knowledge, the teachings on the abhidharma are given. Therefore, corresponding to what needs to be developed on the path, there are three major categories of teachings that are presented in order to enhance one's understanding.

Sutra

The sutric teachings display four characteristics. The first is "place." *Place* means that in a sutra certain characters are mentioned and there is a specific situation that is being presented. The second is "mark," *tsan nyid* in Tibetan. The sutra teachings present the view of the two levels of truth—the mark of the relative truth, how things appear, and the mark of absolute truth, how things exist. The third characteristic is the dharmas, which in this context refers to "entities." The sutric teachings expound on the dharmas, such as the five skandhas, our five psychophysical constituents, our sensory presentations, our mental events. The fourth is "meaning," *don* in Tibetan, which means that the sutras try to convey the intentions of the Buddha.

Abhidharma

Abhidharma teachings also have four characteristics. The first characteristic inclines the practitioner towards enlightenment. The second characteristic trains the person in analysis, in terms of what sort of things exist or do not exist. The third characteristic is that abhidharma teachings can be used in order to overpower one's opponent, that is its literal meaning. The fourth one is that the abhidharma teachings, because they are so detailed, can teach the practitioner how to overcome their doubts and also correct misunderstandings and wrong views that they may be entertaining about existence.

That completes what is called the "Direct Teachings of the Buddha," or *ka* in Tibetan.

Shastras

The shastras are the commentarial literatures based upon Buddha's direct teachings. The shastras must have six major factors or major characteristics inherent in them in order to legitimize the value of the text. Before one commits something to writing, one must be sure that these six different types of characteristics are well respected.

The first factor for shastra literature is that the text should be free of meaningless gibberish, such as one would find in the *Four Vedas*.[3] The text should have proper and unsullied meaning.

With the second factor, the text should be free of tendencies to fall into the extreme views of eternalism or nihilism. This distinguishes Buddhist shastras from non-Buddhist shastras. Numerous commentarial literatures subscribe to an eternal being as the opportunity for release from bondage in order to obtain freedom, which is an anathema to Buddhist literature.

The third factor denotes the importance of the text being free from excessive concern with literary niceties. The shastra should be free of poetic inclinations and obsession with finer points of literacy.

The fourth states that the shastras should be of pure intention and free of sophistry. It should also be free of the intention to degrade other arguments for the purpose of seeking to elevate one's own argument and create an appearance of cleverness.

The fifth factor is that the shastras should be free of interpolation, to ensure the meaning of the teachings is not subverted. For example, scriptural texts such as the Bhagavad Gita can appear to condone violence, and therefore the intention is deceptive.

The sixth factor indicates the shastras should be free of subscribing to views that lead to sacrifice, sacramental activities such as killing or sacrificing animals, or any teachings that involve harm to living creatures, both human and non-human.

There are both Indian and non-Indian shastras. There are shastras written by Nagarjuna,[4] Asanga,[5] and others in India, and there are shastras written by a number of teachers in Tibet. However, one has to be aware that all these six factors need to be observed, and if they are not, then the shastra ceases to be valid from the Buddhist perspective. The text must be compliant to the six factors to be considered valid.

Yana

Yana literally means "vehicle." The nine yana system of the Nyingma tradition is at a slight variance to the more orthodox version which has three yanas—the Hinayana, Mahayana, and Vajrayana.

The first three of the nine yanas are the sutra yanas. The way in which the dharma is practiced generally is by embarking on one of these yanas. The Tibetan word for that is *thegpa*. Thegpa etymologically means "something that would elevate the person." In this particular case, we are referring to elevating oneself from samsaric condition to a much higher level.

The reason why so many yanas are taught is because the dharma is not taught arbitrarily or rigidly. The teachings are always taught in a particular way with immutable method and content, but they are also taught in varieties of ways depending upon the situation, the circumstance, and the audience present.

The first three sutra yanas are basically orientated towards dealing with people of varying capacities.

Sravakayana

The Sravakayana is taught for the people who have very limited vision or capacity. For instance, people who embark on the Sravakayana do not care about others and do not comprehend the notion of benefitting others. However, realizing their present condition is untenable, their motivation to practice is to change the situation they are in. The person realizes that what they perceive to be pleasurable, happy, desirable, and so on, ultimately turns out to be dissatisfactory and unsatisfying. As the sutras say, one feels as though they are being thrown into a huge bonfire. Therefore, there is a desire to make a quick exit, to escape from the dissatisfactory and unsatisfying conditions. So the four noble truths,[6] truth of suffering, truth of the source of suffering, truth of the path, and truth of cessation of suffering, are taught as a main focus within this yana.

The Sravaka practitioner realizes the world is full of suffering and dissatisfaction. Rather than simply learning from their suffering, the practitioner seeks to find out the origin of suffering, what the cause of the suffering is. By doing so, the Sravaka finds out that the suffering comes from within. It is the mind that produces dissatisfaction, anguish, and anxiety. Then, when this is realized, that the suffering is generated by oneself, the practitioner embarks on the path with vigor and more direction. Regular meditation practice is established to try to eradicate defilements, overcome non-virtuous inclinations, and to replace them with virtuous dispositions with the idea of eventually aiming for and finding nirvana. From the Sravaka point of view, nirvana is seen almost as a state of extinction. As it says, truth of cessation means that all one's mental agitations and so forth are put to rest. Therefore, there is a final state of rest, rather than continuous activity. This is quite different to the Mahayana vision of nirvana.

From the Mahayana[7] point of view, the Sravakas are divided into four different types.

The first type is called "Sravakas who manifest even though they are *bodhisattvas,*" *trubye kyi nyin thu* in Tibetan. They are closet bodhisattvas who do not reveal themselves to be bodhisattvas, but pretend that they are Sravakas so that they would be able to mix with and benefit such individuals.

The second type is called *tsudan zhin nyin thu* in Tibetan. The sutras have a number of bodhisattvas, such as *Vajrapani, Avoloketisvara, Manjusri,*[8] and so on. It is said that *Mangoliputra,* who was one of the principal disciples of the Buddha and an apparent Sravaka was considered the incarnation of Vajrapani, Subhuti was an incarnation of Avoloketisvara, and Shariputra was an incarnation of Manjusri, and so on. This is how the mahayanists view the early Sravaka disciples of the Buddha. Tsudan zhin nyin thu means that even though these Sravakas are not full blown bodhisattvas, nonetheless they have taken the bodhisattva vow.

There are two different types of bodhisattva vows. In the first vow, one aspires to become a bodhisattva, in the second, one enters into the bodhisattva path. These Sravakas are actually amateur bodhisattvas. Even though they are actually practicing the Sravaka path, they should essentially be regarded as bodhisattvas.

The third type are "Sravakas who have actually come to the end of their career," *tenzinpa* in Tibetan. These Sravakas are about to be woken up to the reality that arahathood is not the final resting point at all. They recognize the need to embark on the bodhisattva path in order to become fully enlightened.

The fourth type is called *jun zhinpa yinthur* in Tibetan. Jun zhinpa yinthur means people who are not necessarily practitioners but who subscribe to the Hinayana philosophy, such as the philosophy of the *vibaishakas* or *sautantrikas*.[9] *Jun* means philosophy, *zhinpa* means to hold, or to subscribe to. These people may not even be practitioners but their intellectual inclination has to do with the Sravaka teachings. The etymological meaning of Sravaka is "the hearers," and it may also be suggested that many of the Sravakas may in fact not be great practitioners, but they have listened to teachings and may have certain intellectual inclination towards a certain form of teachings.

Pratyekabuddhayana

The second yana is called the *Pratyekabuddhayana*, which is translated as "solitary realizer." They are called solitary realizer as it is said these practitioners do not need any teachers. They come into the world and then through their own effort are able to attain arahathood.[10] They automatically gain some intuitive understanding of the workings of the "*twelve nidanas*," or "twelve links of interdependent origination." By simply looking at death, the practitioner can infer death comes from old age; old age comes from birth; birth comes from grasping, grasping comes from craving; craving comes from feeling, feeling comes from contact; contact comes from sensory presentations, sensory presentations come from the body and mind; body and mind come from consciousness, consciousness comes from volition; and volition comes from ignorance.

By looking at the workings of the twelve nidanas, the solitary realizer can realize that everything, all the human experiences, actually arise out of ignorance, and that ignorance is the root and the cause of all the suffering. Therefore, by contemplating on impermanence and suffering, the person is again prompted to work on it and to gain realization of the non-substantiality of the samsaric condition, and again, attain nirvana as a result of that. The Sravakayana and the Pratyekabuddhayana comprise what is generally known as Hinayana.

Mahayana

Mahayana is known as the "approach of purification." Through the practice of Mahayana, we endeavor to purify varieties of passions and emotional disturbances by generating what is called *bodhichitta*, which is fundamentally the development of compassion. The orientation of the practitioner is not towards renunciation, but rather of purifying one's consciousness and also expanding oneself into the social environment, in relation to helping others. The idea of the bodhisattva is such an important concept because as a mahayanist, we are supposed to participate in the world. We live with others in an intra-subjective world, therefore the best approach is to help others as much as we can, and not just be focused on our own path. Such an act itself is seen as a purification process for us to eventually develop bodhicitta.

There is also the view in Mahayana that there is a certain spiritual element within ourselves that has never been corrupted by our passions, emotional turmoils, and so forth, which is called "Buddha-nature." There is that potential for awakening if we allow ourselves. Given the opportunity, we could work with that potentiality and become enlightened. In terms of meditation, the approach is to purify our emotional disturbance through understanding emptiness, or insubstantiality, *sunyata*. We can realize the insubstantiality of our emotional experiences by contemplating emptiness. Also, through building the mental dexterity that recognizes that mental and emotional events are insubstantial and thus changeable, we are able to replace certain negative emotions with positive ones. For example, in order to overcome anger, we could contemplate on an object that would incite and generate love or compassion instead of anger.

The Mahayana is distinguished from the Sravaka and Prateyekabuddha yanas in a number of ways. As the Mahayana sutra *Alankara* says,

> "The practitioners of the Mahayana, the people who have
> embarked on the Mahayana vehicle, due to their
> transcendental knowledge, do not abide in the *samsara*.
> Due to compassion they do not reside in nirvana either.
> Therefore they do not abide either in nirvana nor samsara."

So the mahayanists' vision is quite different to that of the Sravakas and the Pratyekabuddhas. The mahayanist's aim is not to escape from samsara and leave it behind to aim for nirvana, nor devalue samsara and attach enormous importance to nirvanic aspirations.

Instead of seeing suffering, our passions and emotions, and the condition we are in as real or solid and substantial, something that we need to escape from or reject, we see that we can purify these experiences through contemplating and understanding the concept of emptiness. So the mahayanist recognizes the insubstantiality of their suffering, such as emotional afflictions and rigid ways of thinking, and therefore their desire to escape from samsara is diminished. Consequently, they want to work for the benefit of others, which is what the bodhisattva ideal is.

There is a distinction between how one is now, relative bodhicitta, and what one is aspiring to be, absolute bodhicitta. It is said, someone who has generated relative bodhicitta is thinking of making a journey to arrive at a particular destination. Whereas, someone generating absolute bodhicitta has already taken the journey. Therefore, a mahayanist is still trying to achieve an ideal state in order to work for the benefit of others.

Seven Factors that Distinguish the Mahayana from the Hinayana

The first five factors are pertinent to the path and the next two relate to the fruition stages.

The first factor that distinguishes the Mahayana from the Hinayana is called "the vision," *migpa* in Tibetan. Migpa means the bodhisattva, the practitioner of the Mahayana's vision is to understand the meaning of the bodhisattvic activity. The vision is not limited to arahathood.

The second factor is "aspirations," or *dunpa* in Tibetan. The aspiration of the bodhisattva is to benefit all sentient beings, not just to attain release or emancipation from samsara for themselves.

The third is "wisdom," or *yeshe* in Tibetan. Through the cultivation of wisdom, the bodhisattva is able to understand emptiness, the insubstantiality of both self and other. The Sravakas have understood the emptiness of self, but not the emptiness of the other, the emptiness of phenomena.

The fourth is "great effort," or *tsondus* in Tibetan. In this context, great effort refers to the bodhisattvas displaying enormous endurance. The bodhisattva is not in a hurry to attain nirvana as are the Sravakas, who feel that samsara is like a bonfire that they want to escape from as quickly as possible. Instead, the bodhisattva has enormous endurance and patience, as they want to remain in samsara until all the other sentient beings are transported to a state of enlightenment.

The fifth is "skillful means," or *thab la khas pa* in Tibetan. Skillful means signifies that the bodhisattva is not fixated on one type of approach or solution, set of formulas, or an absolute doctrine. Rather, due to the skillful nature of the bodhisattva intention, they are able to be inclusive. By not remaining in either samsara or nirvana, the bodhisattva is able to not let go of sentient beings and equally, not let their practice suffer. If the bodhisattvas were only desiring nirvana, then the sentient beings would be forgotten. If the bodhisattva were completely engrossed in benefiting sentient beings, then their aspiration to become enlightened would suffer. The bodhisattva is able to accomplish these two tasks simultaneously.

The sixth factor refers to the bodhisattva being endowed with the greater power of the Buddha, *yang dag dunpa* in Tibetan. When the bodhisattva becomes Buddha, becomes fully enlightened, then even more spiritual powers begin to manifest so that the capacity to benefit others would increase exponentially.

The seventh factor, through becoming a Buddha, the bodhisattva is able to engage in unceasing Buddha activity for the benefit of others, *thrinlas* in Tibetan. It's not the case, as with the arahat, that once you have attained arahathood, then all activity would cease, but rather, the bodhisattva would continue to benefit sentient beings until the end of samsara, which is forever.

In the Mahayana, the "Great Vehicle" system, there are two accumulations to enhance the practitioner on the path— accumulation of merit and accumulation of wisdom. Accumulation of merit is accomplished through practicing the *Six Paramitas* or "six transcendental perfections"—generosity, discipline, patience, vigor, meditation, and wisdom. The accumulation of wisdom is accomplished through the cultivation of transcendental knowledge, which is the analytical meditation whereby one realizes the nature of things as being empty or insubstantial.

The mahayanist view is also unlike that of the Sravakas as their view is substantialist. The non-substantialist view in Mahayana is established through realizing the interdependent nature of the two truths—relative truth and absolute truth. The view has to be dependent on the two levels of truths and the fruition of Mahayana practice is to realize two aspects of Buddha's being—the aspect of the form and the aspect of the formless. Basically, that sums up the three sutra yanas—the Sravakayana, Prateyekabhuddhayana, and the Mahayana.

Vajrayana

Having discussed the three yana system of the Sutrayana—the Sravakayana, the Pratayekabuddhayana, and the Mahayana—we now come to the tantric approach, also known as Vajrayana. The tantric approach is called "the path of transformation," a contrast to the path of renunciation where one may be required to reject certain things seen as not conducive to spiritual discipline. In contrast, with the Vajrayana approach, one transforms the energies of negativity and uses them in order to further one's spiritual growth. The tantric approach is also different to the Mahayana where the practitioner attempts to purify themselves through the development of bodhicitta and through the understanding of emptiness.

In the tantric approach, the practitioner not only sees the insubstantiality of their emotions, but also a basic, subsisting energy within the emotions. One tries to transform or transmute negative emotions, known as the "five poisons," into much more enhancing forms of psychic, life enhancing energy. The five poisons of desire, aggression, jealousy, pride, and ignorance are transformed or transmuted, into their corresponding five wisdoms.

Desire is transformed into discriminating wisdom, aggression into mirror-like wisdom, jealousy into all-accomplishing wisdom, pride into wisdom of equanimity, and ignorance into wisdom of *dharmadhatu*, or reality.

That is why the language of alchemy is used a lot of the time in tantric literature. Just as alchemists turn lead into gold, in the same way, the practitioner is supposed to turn all the base, undesirable negative materials into something positive, sublime, and spiritual.

In the tantric system, negative emotions are considered inherent to one's samsaric nature and not necessarily conducive towards spiritual growth in their current form. Therefore, these emotions need to be transformed, or converted into something much more enhancing, something much more positive.

The Outer Tantras

The first three yanas related with Tantra are kriya, charya, and yoga, and are known as the "outer tantras." They are called the outer tantras because they emphasize the use of signs or symbols, *tsan ma* in Tibetan. The emphasis is on visualization of a deity or a particular implement, such as a *vajra*, a sword, and so on, and also the use of *mantras* and syllables. The inner tantras do not place emphasis on sign or symbols so much and are therefore called tsan ma medpa, meaning "signless."

In the outer tantras, particularly kriya and charya, the practitioner approaches the deity with the expectation of being rewarded, wanting both temporal and spiritual benefit from the practice. The practitioner's concern may include wishing to avoid sickness, to become wealthy and prosperous, to experience progress on the spiritual path, and so on. Thus, one is thinking of reward.

In the inner tantras, that is not the case. One does not visualize deities or practice because of a desire to be rewarded by a deity. One no longer considers the deity to be anything separate from oneself. However, at the beginning stages of Tantra, the outer tantras, one experiences the manifestation of the deity as separate to oneself and wishes to have certain needs fulfilled.

The tantric method is regared as more expedient to sutric methods. The tantric method, generally, is called *katsik mepa* in Tibetan, meaning "without hardship." However, as people who practice Tantra have discovered, it is not totally without hardship.

The reason why the tantric approach is considered easier is that it is designed to deal with our emotions more directly, transforming negative aspects into a much more positive and spiritually fulfilling state. This is done through the use of visualizations, mantras, and other ritual practices. It is said that if one approaches the inner tantras properly, one can attain enlightenment in one lifetime.

The tantric method is designed to uncover our samsaric mind, leaving nothing hidden. There are many methods and there is no such thing as one approach because there are many different ways to visualize, recite mantras, and conduct rituals.

It is generally not full of hardship as with the sutric approach, often referred to as the gradual approach. Tantra is seen as more instantaneous. Normally, the practitioner is required to do preliminary practices in preparation for Tantra. This is done to refine the intellect and purify one's intention to help the practitioner to directly experience the teachings. From the nine yana point of view, it is said that the Hinayana motivation is self focused, the Mahayana approach is encompassing, and that Tantra requires a more intelligent and insightful approach.

The View and Approach of the Three Outer Tantras

Kriya, *jawa* in Tibetan, literally means "action." Kriya emphasizes physicality, how one should conduct oneself when interacting with others and how one should conduct rituals. Precision in conducting the rituals is emphasized, there is less emphasis on meditation and on the mental aspect. The second one is charya, and emphasizes body and speech. The emphasis is on the mudras and the utterance of mantras, and the coordination of these two, but not as much emphasis is placed on the mind. The third is yoga, where the mind is emphasized and seen as the primary focus. The mudras and mantras are less emphasized in this yana.

When the practitioner of kriya tantra visualizes the deity, they have to realize that the absolute truth and the relative truth are not in conflict with each other, but are intimately related. The visualization of the deity is not used in order to reveal a divine identity, but rather seeing that the divinity itself is the embodiment of the two truths. As the deity is visualized and thus insubstantial in nature, it represents absolute truth. Still, the visualized deity has presence—a certain form, color, characteristics, and so on, which indicates the relative truth. So the practice of visualization is conducted in order to acquaint the practitioner with this relationship between the two truths. As it has been said, "The two truths, absolute and relative truth, have never been separated from the beginning, and this is the ultimate view of all tantras." It has also been said, "The absolute, which is unconditioned, manifests as the conditioned. However, the conditioned itself has no ultimate reality; it therefore manifests as the deity. For that reason they cannot be separated."

By adopting that attitude of the inseparability of the two truths, without letting the mind be agitated, one usually begins the *sadhana* or the practice, with the mantra of emptiness, *om sobava shudo dharma svabhava shudo hum*.

When one visualizes the deity, first of all, one empties the world of all contents and empties one's mind of all contents so there is only emptiness present with no image, nothing. That emptiness represents the *dharmakaya*; it's called "the deity of dharmakaya."

The utterance of the mantra, the sound of the mantra, om sobava shudo dharma svabhava shudo hum, is called "the deity of the sound." After uttering the mantra, one visualizes a particular seed syllable, whether it's a "hung" or another seed syllable, which visually manifests, then this transforms itself into the deity, such as *Prajnaparamita*, called "the body deity." The use of the deity in Tantra has to do with deification or sanctification of one's whole experience.

In terms of conduct, the kriya tantra practitioner would usually refrain from eating meat, consuming alcohol, and would practice good personal hygiene. Those are the conditions within which the kriya yoga is practiced.

In a brief summary of charya tantra, it can be seen as not very different from the kriya yoga practice. The difference in approach comes with the visualization: one visualizes oneself as the deity, and a replica of that deity is then invited to manifest in front of oneself at one's eyebrow level. Light radiates from the seed syllable visualized at the heart center or chakra; the light travels out, making offerings. The light is enriched and energized and returns to the practitioner who becomes empowered from the light.

Yoga tantra is the final phase of the outer tantra practices. It is differentiated from the other two with the emphasis no longer on cleanliness or conduct. As stated earlier, the emphasis in yoga tantra is on the mind. In this particular context, the practitioner does not think in terms of purity because one is visualized as the deity and thus already pure. When engaging in the visualization practice, unlike in the kriya and charya tantras, one does not have to stop the mind from wandering. One simply lets the mind be as it is then one visualizes a seed syllable, such as AH. The letter AH, for example, then transforms into a moon disk, and then another seed syllable, such as HUNG, would appear on the moon disk. Light would then radiate from the HUNG in all directions, making offerings to the Buddhas and bodhisattvas, and when it re-enters the practitioner's body, the HUNG transforms into a five-pronged vajra. The five-pronged vajra eventually transforms into one of the *dhyani* Buddhas, such as *Samantabhadra*. One visualizes the deity outside of oneself as the replica of the deity, which enters into one's body. The practitioner has total identification with the deity. In the previous two tantras of kriya and charya, the deity one visualized oneself as being, the samayasattva, and its replica outside of oneself, the jnanasattva, remain distinct. On the yoga tantra stage, there is a union of the two.

In yoga tantra, one is not forbidden to eat meat and so on. It is also said that in terms of conduct, one should no longer be thinking totally in terms of dualism, seeing certain things as acceptable and certain other things as not acceptable. While naturally having developed a non-harming attitude, the practitioner should be conducting their life in a much freer and spontaneous way.

Mahayoga and anuyoga belong to the inner circle of the tantras. In mahayoga and anuyoga, the practice is oriented towards working with the internal psychic energy pathways. That is to say, in these yogas, we are trying to transform our base emotions into wisdom.

The outlook of the practitioner of mahayoga is to keep three things in mind—*dondam*, *kunzop*, and *yermed* in Tibetan. Dondam means absolute truth, kunzop means relative truth, and yermed means non-divisibility of the two. Gradually, as the practitioner engages in the practices through the visualization of deities, mandalas, recitation of mantras, and so on, the practitioner begins to increasingly realize that the nature of the deity is self-awareness wisdom or absolute truth and also, that there is no difference between the deity and the self-awareness wisdom of the mind. The practitioner also begins to realize that relative truth is none other than the variety of their experiences—happiness, unhappiness, desire, passion of all kinds, and so forth. These unceasing experiential manifestations that arise in our minds are seen as not being different from the self-awareness wisdom, absolute truth. It is not the case that we have our defilements and impurities in one bag, and wisdom, insight and knowledge in another. All these varieties of mental experiences are seen as manifestation of self-awareness wisdom.

It is said by perceiving the relative in this way, we are able to appreciate the five psychophysical constituents instead of degrading them, instead of saying, "My body is a product of karma, my mind is deluded, and my volition, my concepts, are a product of karma, and therefore something that needs to be negated and gotten rid of." Instead, one begins to see the five psychophysical constituents and the five sense fields as the mandala itself, the *mandala* of the deity. So there is a deification process taking place in relation to how one sees oneself.

As mentioned, yermed means non-duality, or non-divisibility, of the two truths. As discussed, that means that one no longer views absolute and relative truth as separate. Even if there may be some kind of dualism present, through effective practice, dualistic thinking can eventually be eradicated. The absolute and relative are always co-existent and co-present. The absolute does not chronologically precede the relative. The relative and the absolute are always conjoined.

As it has been said,

"The unconditioned itself has manifested as the conditioned. So to see the relative in the proper mode, in its proper existential mode, is to see the absolute. Even though they may be perceived to be distinct and may seem to hold some kind of relationship of cause and effect, nonetheless that is only apparent, it is not real. One cannot see the relationship between absolute and relative as the relationship founded on cause and effect."

Anuyoga, *naljor lamey* in Tibetan, is a further extension of mahayoga. The difference between mahayoga and anuyoga is that in mahayoga, the emphasis is on the development stage of practice, *kyerim* in Tibetan, *sampattikrama* in Sanskrit. So the emphasis is on the visualization of the deities and the precision of how they are visualized. As previously described, the process of building the visualization is normally done in stages. For example, we may first begin by visualizing a seed syllable that turns into a moon disc and a second seed syllable is visualized that turns into the deity, or an aspect of the deity, such as an implement. The visualization process continues until all the details are incorporated into the visualization. In anuyoga, the emphasis is on the fulfillment stage, *zogrim* in Tibetan, *sampannakrama* in Sanskrit. One no longer concerns oneself with the details of the visualizations.

With anuyoga practice, the practitioner develops an attitude of non-separability of the authentic aspect of one's physical being and the wisdom aspect, seen as the authentic dimension of the mind, realizing that those two aspects are inseparable and that those two dimensions have been pure right from the beginning. It is considered that one's body, in its authentic state, and the mind, have ultimately never been defiled. By adopting that attitude, then one engages in the practice of visualization, recitation of mantras, and so on. Unlike the previous practices, in the anuyoga system, one visualizes the deity instantaneously. We no longer build the visualization up gradually from seed syllables. We visualize the deity as complete, spontaneously, on the spot, with the throne, all the implements, and so forth.

Realization of the Five Aspects of the Body

As a result of the practice of anuyoga, it is said one realizes the five aspects of the physical body, *kuna* in Tibetan.

The first aspect is called "the existential aspect of the body," *ngo wo nyid sku* in Tibetan, *svabhavavikakaya* in Sanskrit, which means the body in its natural state, free of mental concepts and ideas and so forth.

The second aspect is "the expression of the body as undiluted and unpolluted," *chos ku* in Tibetan, dharmakaya in Sanskrit.

The third aspect is often translated as "body of bliss," *long chod zog pa'i ku* (*long ku*) in Tibetan, *sambhogakaya* in Sanskrit. When a person is free from defilements and obscurations, one is able to experience a state of bliss.

The fourth aspect is the physical expression that manifests perceptibly, in terms of benefiting others, benefitting both those who are pure and proper in their conduct, and those who are defiled and are ignorant. Which is *tulku* in Tibetan, *nirmanakaya* in Sanskrit.

The fifth aspect is called "mystery body," which means that all these different dimensions and the expressions of the body are united in the most fundamental, inexplicable way. The mystery body is hidden from our normal ways of thinking and is not subject to discussions, language, et cetera, but is the dimension that provides the ground for the cohesiveness for all the other dimensions of the body.

Realization of the Five Aspects of Speech

The second realization that comes from anuyoga practice is the realization of speech, *sung* in Tibetan.

The first aspect is the "Speech of the Existential Being," which has to be heard in an inarticulate way—unuttered, unarticulated. The Speech of the Existential Being is not something that is put into words and then heard, it is more felt. The meaning of the whole thing is conveyed with the way you pick up on your feelings, but is not articulated and expressed in words.

The second aspect is the "speech of the dharmakaya." This way of communication is conducted through inspirations. Again, it has nothing to do with written or spoken words.

The third aspect is the "speech of the sambhogakaya, *long ku'i sung* in Tibetan. The speech of the sambhogakaya is communicated through intentions, mentally. Again, it is not conveyed through words.

The fourth one is the "speech of the mystery body," the mystery dimension of the being, *sun me koya sung* in Tibetan. This is communicated through the use of varieties of gestures and signs. Once again, the conveyance does not rely on words.

The fifth one is the "speech of the nirmanakaya," *trul ku'i sung* in Tibetan. The nirmanakaya communicates through words but in the most profound, poetic, and eloquent manner.

Realization of the Five Aspects of Mind

The third realization that comes from anuyoga practice is the aspect of mind, *thug* in Tibetan, and this also has five aspects.

The first is that the nature of the mind, which is empty, manifests as the "wisdom of dharmakaya," *chos ying namdag yeshe* in Tibetan which has no shape or color or form. It has no content, no thoughts, no ideas or anything of the sort. It is a total state of openness.

The second aspect is "mirror-like wisdom," *melong ta bu'i yeshe* in Tibetan. Mirror-like wisdom refers to the mind in its natural state, completely undiluted, unpolluted, unvitiated, and unsullied. It is totally pure, translucent, and clear.

The third aspect of the mind is the "wisdom of equanimity," *nyam pa nyid yeshe* in Tibetan. This aspect of the mind has the ability to view everything with a sense of equality. It does not judge certain things to be undesirable and have aversion towards them, or judge other things to be something to be cultivated and developed.

The fourth aspect is "wisdom of analysis" or "analytical wisdom," *sor tog yeshe* in Tibetan. Even though one views everything as being equal, one identifies diversity and difference. There is no denial or confusion in recognizing distinctions that exist among varieties of categories of thought and existence.

The fifth aspect is "wisdom of accomplishment," *ja drub yeshe* in Tibetan. Without having to exert oneself, without deliberation, one would be able to accomplish things spontaneously because one is no longer restrained by a variety of fears, apprehensions, and doubts normally associated with our ordinary ways of thinking.

Through the practice of anuyoga, one is able to eventually come to the optimum experience of the purified state of body, speech, and mind, and the unity of these three. That is considered the ultimate achievement of the whole process of Tantra. Anuyoga tantra is thus the stepping stone to enter into Dzogchen, or *Maha Ati* practice, which is treated as going beyond Tantra, because in Dzogchen there is no need for visualizations, recitation of mantras, and other ritual practices.

Atiyoga Yana—Dzogchen

Up to this point, I have discussed the Buddhist path from the graduated or gradual point of view, related in some respect with lam rim or "graduated path." Within the graduated path is the notion that one is trying to achieve something, working towards a particular goal, eliminating or eradicating confusions or defilements, and clearing obscurations using different practices and other methods.

In summary, from the Hinayana point of view, that of the Sravakas and Pratyekabuddhas, the approach to the practice is that of renunciation. The person approaches the practice with the intention to eradicate their ignorance, desire, anger, jealousy, bitterness, and so on. From the Mahayana point of view, with the development of the concept of emptiness or insubstantiality, and the notions of the two truths, one is trying to understand that everything is insubstantial by nature. In Mahayana, there is still an effort involved in terms of dealing with what is negative and what is undesirable, which is accomplished through purification. Within the tantric practices, one engages in ritual practices—visualization of deities and recitation of mantras, and so on—with the intention to transform or transmute one's negative qualities into positive qualities, with the intention to attain Buddhahood.

The first eight yanas deal with the ordinary, everyday consciousness, whereas the ninth one, Dzogchen, or *Maha Ati*, deals with one's existential being. *Zogpa chen po* is the Tibetan translation of the Sanskrit word Maha Ati, which literally means "the great ultimate," or "the great fulfillment." Dzog pa means "fulfillment," and chen po means "great," so "great fulfillment." One might ask, "What does that mean, great fulfillment of what?" It refers to the fulfillment of one's full potential. The fundamental idea is that we all have the capacity to become a fully-fledged or fully awakened human being. The discrepancies that exist within oneself are able to be overcome.

From the Dzogchen perspective, all the problems of the so-called samsaric existence have emerged not as any kind of cosmological or metaphysical evolutionary process, but rather as misunderstanding, or misassessment, of what is called one's "primordial condition." Samsara, in this particular context, should be understood as self-estrangement, going astray from one's true condition. The samsaric condition consists of nothing other than a lack of intellectual ignition and lack of awareness.

As the previous yanas have shown, many techniques and methods are utilized. The Dzogchen or Maha Ati point of view is totally different. From the Dzogchen point of view, as soon as one uses a technique to realize or gain something, one has automatically changed, modulated, or in a sense contrived, the original natural state of the mind.

Different Yanas Different Goals

Meditative experience is not something that can be articulated or talked about effectively. However, in order to point out the different techniques and invoke realizations and spiritual experience, there is value in talking about such experiences in particular ways. For that reason, in Buddhist teachings, there are different systems, different viewpoints, and also different practices in keeping with those views. The nine yanas provide alternative approaches that are available for a person who is interested in attaining enlightenment.

These different yanas should remain separate, and should not be seen as leading to the same goal. For example, when a hinayanist embarks on the path, that person has a distinct aspiration in mind. They set a particular goal they want to achieve, and they engage in a particular mode of practice that is only relevant in that context, but it may not be relevant in the context of Mahayana. As with all the yanas, Hinayana practitioners have their own approach and system. They have their own starting point, they have their own idea of the path, and they have their own idea of the goal—*gzhi*, *lam*, and *dras bu* in Tibetan. The attitudes that are developed in the Hinayana are also different from the Mahayana and Tantra.

In the Hinayana, attachment is a primary focus, because it is due to attachment that we have problems with ego clinging, belief in permanence, and so on. In the Hinayana, when a person embarks on the spiritual journey, they generate revulsion and despair to assist in the process of renouncing samsara. Those two are important ingredients on the hinayanist's spiritual path. Without having revulsion to our familiar world, what we call samsara, and despairing that even though we seek happiness, satisfaction, joy, et cetera, we have to come to the realization that unless a different way of achieving those goals is adopted, we will remain frustrated. These two attitudes are essential on this path—revulsion on the one hand, and despair on the other. When the person has developed enough revulsion and despair, then they would want to renounce all that is familiar—to become a spiritual person, one has to have developed a totally radical attitude. There has to be a revolution taking place in the consciousness so that one retreats from the familiar world. For this reason, in the Hinayana perspective, the idea of renunciation is extraordinarily important.

In Mahayana, one is not dealing with attachment alone, but aversion, or anger, because the fundamental concern for the Mahayana practitioner is to benefit others. Therefore, one embarks on the spiritual path not because one wants to become enlightened for oneself, but because if one were able to become enlightened, then one would be able to benefit others more. So in the Mahayana context, the fundamental virtue that one has to cultivate is patience, because from patience comes the ability to develop love, compassion, generosity, and so on. Without patience, one cannot develop any of the other virtues, even if one tries. The fundamental vice is aversion, because as long as aversion is present, then one would not be able to develop patience and all the associated virtues.

Ultimately, the goal of the Mahayana is to realize emptiness, which is to say that finally one begins to realize that even the idea of benefiting others is ultimately insubstantial. When a person practices generosity, patience, compassion, or love, identity becomes less solid, there is a less solid ego. The virtuous deeds are also insubstantial, and the object of virtuous deeds, the people one is trying to benefit, is also insubstantial. In that sense, one has the notion of emptiness pervading that three-term relationship, which is called *khor sum mi tog pa'i yeshe* in Tibetan. Khor sum mi tog pa'i yeshe means that one no longer makes distinction between the subject, the one who is practicing the virtue, the act of the practice of virtue, and the person who is the object of virtue.

In the tantric system, the fundamental goal is to develop wisdom, and wisdom is achieved by working on ignorance. In the Hinayana, one starts with attachment, then in the Mahayana, one works with aversion, or anger, and with the tantric system, one works with ignorance. By working with ignorance, one can realize wisdom. Wisdom is accomplished by transforming one's negative emotions through the use of prescribed tantric practices—visualizing deities, reciting mantras, and so on—so that one begins to make use of the negative emotions in order to realize wisdom. The *tantrika* realizes that there is no conflict, and no need to renounce or purify negativity, as is the case of Hinayana and Mahayana, but they can be transformed.

The Dzogchen, or self-liberation approach, is different from the other approaches because one is no longer working with any specific emotions or trying to do anything specific. The aim of Dzogchen is to be able to remain in the natural state. If one tries to do something, even with the approach of renunciation, or purification, or transformation, then one is already interfering with one's natural state. So the aim of Dzogchen is to realize one's full potential and realize that one's fundamental existential condition is pure, uncorrupted by one's defilements and obscurations. In fact, from the Dzogchen perspective, even the obscurations and defilements are seen as spontaneously established in the context of reality as such. So in this way, there is no real distinction between the starting point, the path, and the goal. In Dzogchen, we can only conceptually make such a distinction between the starting point, which is when we are an ordinary confused human being; the path, which is the gradual realization of our true condition; and the goal, or fruition, which is to realize ourselves as being perfect, and is what Dzogchen means.

That distinction is only a conceptual distinction, there is no real distinction, because in Dzogchen, the goal is already present. The goal is not something that one achieves as a result of effort and is seen as something new. It is not like any of the other yanas. In the other yanas, if you achieve nirvana, it is seen as something new. If you attain *bodhisattvahood*, then that is something new that has been achieved. If you realize yourself as the deity, then you are attaining something new in Tantra. But in Dzogchen, what one discovers is that one's own true condition has been pure and uncorrupted, right from the beginning. In that sense, there is no nirvana to be sought after and there is no samsara to be left behind, because samsara and nirvana are two sides of the same existence.

In that way, we can see the importance of keeping the different approaches distinct, even though there is a thematic continuity running through the whole nine yanas. There is a continuity, yet at the same time, they are quite distinct in intent and in practice, as well as in aspiration.

Sudden and Gradual Relationship

My intention in contrasting Dzogchen with the other yanas was to illustrate that the Dzogchen approach fully supports the idea of instantaneous enlightenment. Though some of the later tantric approaches are more expedient, they are still gradual, not instantaneous. In Dzogchen, the approach is seen as instantaneous or sudden, *cig carwa* in Tibetan, as opposed to gradual, *rim can pa* in Tibetan.

There are a lot of discussions, comparisons, and misunderstandings about sudden and gradual paths—seeing some as more immediate or sudden, and others as more gradual and slower. Such discussions can be resolved when we recognize that every single path is both gradual and sudden. When one has certain insight into things, then that insight occurs quite suddenly. However, in order to have such an insight there would have been a build-up so one could have that insight. So there is no real contradiction. Even in Dzogchen practice, one has to go about doing particular practices and build up one's practice and understanding so that one might have this or that insight. When one does have those insights, it takes place quite suddenly. At different times and in different places, one can have different types of experiences and insights and insights of varying degrees and depth, depending on how much one has been practicing.

As Shantideva says in his Bodhicharyavatara,[11] "depending on the attitudes of the yogis, the superior yogis would surpass that of the lesser ones." Not all practitioners of Dzogchen who have had insight into their authentic condition are on equal ground. Even if one has had such an experience, that does not mean that one will not have emotional upheavals, doubts about one's practice, or certain suspicions about insights that one has gained. These experiences and doubts are highly likely. It is not just because one has gained certain insight into Dzogchen that all of a sudden one has this inimitable, complete conviction. One can still have doubts or suspicions about one's understanding, one's insights, and yet experienced genuine insight. That is quite important to remember because usually we tend to think that if one has had genuine spiritual insight, that person must have total conviction without a shadow of doubt. It depends on how much insight one has had. It takes a long time to have absolute insight into Dzogchen. However, right from the beginning, one can have varying degrees of insight into Dzogchen, even at the start of practice.

Relative and Absolute Dzogchen

Dzogchen is not considered a school of thought as such, within or outside of Buddhism. Dzogchen means "great fulfillment," or "great completion." In this context, great completion does not indicate we were incomplete but now have become complete. It is not that we have been wandering and drifting around, then suddenly we discovered our true nature, our authentic condition, and therefore we have become a complete person. Rather, according to Dzogchen, we all participate in what is called the authentic condition, *nyur ma nas pa* in Tibetan. *Nyur ma* means authentic, unchanged, uncontrived. *Nas pa* means to exist, to dwell.

Fundamentally, the Dzogchen notion is that whether we know

it or not, we have always existed in that authentic condition. It is seen as a way of existing, or being, rather than a concept or ideal that one must try to develop. The discussion around Dzogchen is focused on ways in which one can go about trying to discover the authentic condition. Therefore, we can say that there are two types of Dzogchen—one is the real authentic condition that one must discover, and the other is the approach or philosophy of Dzogchen, which prescribes certain methods in order to realize that authentic condition. Therefore, we could say that there is absolute Dzogchen and relative Dzogchen.

Relative Dzogchen has to do with our varying experiences in relation to our experience of the authentic condition. One person's level of understanding of their authentic condition may not be the same as another person's level of understanding, and is therefore varied and relative. However, as far as the authentic condition itself is concerned, what is called Dzogchen, there is no difference at all.

In Dzogchen practice, one is trying to attune to one's authentic condition, a condition which one has drifted away from and become disassociated from, a condition which has remained hidden or concealed. The practice is designed to un-conceal or reveal one's true condition. The way in which one goes about this discovery is principally through acknowledgement: recognizing that one has certain undesirable characteristics; and, that one possesses varieties of uncontrolled passions. Instead of suppressing or ignoring these discrepancies, one takes the first step called "acknowledgement." One must recognize that which is undesirable. Without such recognition, one has absolutely no way of dealing with and addressing them.

When one begins to acknowledge the variety of unpleasant experiences, one then starts to develop a certain sense of awareness, called *rigpa* in Dzogchen. Rigpa relates to that process of acknowledgement. When we acknowledge that certain sullied characteristics are present, we can develop true awareness or rigpa. Otherwise, we cannot at all. One has to start off by coming to terms with certain inner tendencies, emotional disturbances, neglected and suppressed feelings, contrived ideas, and so forth. That is the starting point to enable us to work with our true condition.

The Four Misconceptions

There is a transition of attitude that takes place from the normal Buddhist understanding to that of Dzogchen. From the level of Dzogchen, the so called "four misconceptions" are radically changed and understood very differently.

There are generally four misconceptions within the Buddhist discipline:

1. Everything that we perceive is dirty and something that has to be disposed of.
2. What we might regard as pleasure is nothing but disguised pain or suffering. Even though we might think we are experiencing pleasure, we are not experiencing pleasure at all. It is pain, which is mistakenly perceived as pleasure.
3. Everything is impermanent and nothing remains the same.
4. The non-existence of ego. There is no such thing as ego because everything is impermanent, so therefore there is no ego.

However, in Dzogchen the four misconceptions are turned around to be seen as completely the opposite.

1. Everything that we perceive is pure.
2. Everything we experience is pleasure.
3. Everything has a sense of permanency.
4. There is ego.

This might come as a shock to Buddhists because how could Dzogchenpas say such a thing if they claim to be Buddhist? The Dzogchen explanation considers our ordinary understanding of these things as mistaken. It does not mean there is no such thing as pleasure, or there is no such thing as permanence, or there is no such thing as bliss. However, from the Dzogchen point of view, the way that we perceive the ordinary world is completely mistaken.

Looked at from the Dzogchen perspective, the four misconceptions are seen in a totally different manner. The sense of ego is there because there is transcendental consciousness. Because there is transcendental ego, there is permanence, because the transcendental aspect of our self does not go through change. If it did go through change, it would fall into the domain of the relative, not the absolute. Therefore, it does not go through change, and therefore there is a sense of permanence. The world we see changes but the actuality, the reality itself, does not go through change, so there is a sense of permanence. The sense of pleasure is there because once one begins to understand oneself and one's true being, one begins to experience all-pervasive pleasure, which is not the sort of pleasure one normally seeks. What we normally perceive might not be pure, but when our perception radically changes and we begin to see things differently, we see things as being pure and being in the right place, so we do not find any conflict in the way we go about things and the way that we see things. These are extremely important concepts in Dzogchen thought.

Ordinary and Transcendental Consciousness

Within the Dzogchen tradition, it is perceived to be of paramount importance to be able to distinguish between our ordinary consciousness or mind, and the transcendental consciousness or mind-in-itself. These are not so much two different types of consciousness or mind, or different levels of mind, but rather it is mind that is the same, but used in a different way. The mind that we are normally aware of has the capacity to retain memories, and is also the sub-stratum of our traces and dispositions. The transcendental consciousness, or mind-in-itself, is basic awareness which is free from our memory, traces, and dispositions, and is also completely free from our past conditioning and habitual mode of perceiving things. It is also free of future expectations, in terms of how we wish things to be or how we want things to turn out. The capacity to be able to be aware of the moment by moment process that goes on within the mind, free of any judgments, and without using our conceptual categorization, is the transcendental consciousness, or mind-in-itself.

The reason why we are unable to see the moment by moment process that goes on in the mind is because we have a fundamental resistance towards seeing things in their proper mode. In our usual conceptual way of operating, we all have a particular sort of standard way of seeing things. Therefore, there is a general consensus in terms of what we should see, and what we should not see. If you begin to see things differently, then people think you have gone crazy, or that something terrible has happened to you. Therefore, a sense of courage is extremely important to be able to see from another perspective, a perspective that is different from the conventional way of perceiving. We have this general illusion being created which encourages each other's illusions in terms of what we see. Generally, we live in that kind of world, where each other's illusion is being continuously encouraged so that we don't have to see the real, actual situation.

We need to be able to suspend our judgment so that we are not conditioned by our habitual process. Suspending judgment in itself involves overcoming our karmic tendencies. Karma is nothing other than the traces and dispositions that we have accumulated over a period of time, and as a result, it shapes our thinking, it schematizes our way of perceiving things. Therefore, we need to be able to suspend our conventional way of thinking so that we are able to see things in a new light. In order to make this transition, we need to develop basic awareness. Basic awareness is differentiated from our ordinary consciousness mainly because basic awareness has no history. With basic awareness, we are just simply aware of something instead of seeing something judgmentally, comparing and contrasting, et cetera. When we compare and contrast, we are using predetermined ideas and conventional standards, so when we do not compare or contrast, then we are immediately present with whatever it is. That is what basic awareness is. It is free from memory and free from history. It is an ahistorical process of awareness. That is why it is differentiated from our ordinary mode of perceiving, which is historical and is conditioned by external and internal factors. Whereas, basic awareness is not conditioned, it is simply present.

From the Dzogchen perspective, we try to be in the moment, that is, un-divisively or unified, remaining in the dynamic process as much as possible. At least for a period of time, we can try to suspend all our conventional ways of perceiving ourselves and others. Instead of using the conventional standard of categorizing things—ego, self, emotions, passions, and so forth—one tries to be more present and in relationship with what is actually going on. As soon as we start to categorize, we have removed ourselves that much more from the actual experience. So the difference between reality and illusion is that the reality is that which is already present, just simply there. The illusion is created when we perceive that reality through a pre-established pattern of thinking. This obscuration inhibits our ability to see the way things actually exist.

Generally, in Buddhist philosophy, the consciousness is seen as one particular stream that persists through lifetimes. It is the notion of a dynamic consciousness that goes through processes, and consciousness is seen as impermanent and momentary. When a person starts to meditate and purify their karmic dispositions, then some kind of fundamental change in the process of consciousness begins to take place, so that the person becomes more enlightened, or realized.

In Dzogchen, it is slightly different. It is not that our momentary consciousness goes through some type of transformation and becomes something else, being the enlightened state of mind. Rather, in Dzogchen, the person begins to understand that there is a difference between ordinary consciousness and transcendental consciousness. The transcendental consciousness is recognized as atemporal. Concepts such as time and space cannot be attributed to it. It is totally beyond conceptualization. However, the ordinary process of consciousness can be discussed.

Chapter Three

Consciousness and Wisdom
in Yogacara and Dzogchen

The Eight Levels of Consciousness in Yogacara

The description of consciousness in the Dzogchen tradition is largely borrowed from the Yogacara[12] system, also known as *citta matra* meaning "mind only," or *vijnanavada* meaning "doctrine of consciousness." It is one of two major schools of Indian Mahayana Buddhism, the other being *Madhyamaka*. The founders of Yogacara, Asanga and his half brother Vasubandhu, believed Madhyamaka leaned too closely to nihilism by overemphasizing the emptiness of phenomena. Yogacara, meaning "one who practices yoga," is based on the third turning of the wheel by the Buddha and emphasizes the reality of the mind and Buddha-nature.

There is an unconscious level, which is the locus of our preserved karmic reservoir. All our actions and thought processes leave all kinds of impressions and traces in the unconscious level. We may not be aware of them, but still, they exist. We need to see them not as static impressions and traces lurking around in the unconscious, but rather as dispositions that go through continuous change and transformation.

These karmic dispositions are known as *bag chags* in Tibetan. Etymologically, bag chags is very interesting. *Bag* means concealed, hidden, and *chags* means existing, so existing in a concealed manner.

We are not aware of it, we are not aware of our bag chags. If we were, we would not be going about things the way we do, because then we would know what bag chags gives rise to, what sort of action. Bag chags are responsible for all our actions, the way we perceive things, the way we interact with other human beings, the way in which we perceive reality, and the way in which we construct reality. According to Dzogchen, it is this level of consciousness that is largely responsible for constructing the notion of subject and object. All the materials that we gather in order to have this perception of the world we see, and our perception of ourselves, is all drawn from the level of unconscious.

Dzogchenpas would say that the ordinary world we experience is not really the way it is. They believe the way we experience the world is largely constructed from the materials in the unconscious: our belief in the objectivity of the world; that the world exists as separate from us; that the objective world has some type of immutable existence. All these beliefs are constructed by our karmic dispositions and conceptual assumptions of all kinds, which are largely unconscious. All those activities can be seen as pre-conscious. Our perception of the duality of subject and object, and other dualistic notions come about because of the unconscious.

The first six levels of consciousness are comprised of the five sense consciousnesses, and the sixth consciousness, which gives order to what we experience through the senses. When we visually perceive something, we don't just perceive it as some kind of blotch, we perceive it as a tree, a chair, or a person, et cetera. Even when we are hallucinating, or even when we are subjected to some kind of illusion, we see it as something. That is to say, the sixth consciousness puts order to what we hear, visually perceive, smell, taste, and touch. There is some sort of coherence about the workings of the consciousness. If there were no consciousness to organize our experiences into some kind of order, then it would be chaotic. We would not be able to coordinate what we are hearing, smelling, perceiving, or seeing properly. The sixth consciousness puts order to the experience of the sense consciousnesses so we can see the relationship between those levels of consciousness.

The seventh level of consciousness is known as the "egocentric mentation," *manovijnana* in Sanskrit, *yid* in Tibetan. At this level of consciousness, the person is completely conscious of oneself, the other, and the world. Every single experience that one has is interpreted in reference to oneself. Our experiences are interrupted by our sense of self, so the world is seen and experienced from *my* perspective, *my* emotions are perceived from *my* perspective, and *my* feelings are perceived from *my* perspective. I interact with other people from *my* perspective. Everything is experienced in relation to *myself*. We give an interpretation of the basic data that is received though the senses in a self-centered way. Therefore, some kind of distortion of what is actually being perceived begins to take place because of the obsession we have with ourselves being the reference point.

The eighth level is the unconscious which can be translated as "sub-stratum of awareness," "fundamental consciousness," and has also been translated as "storehouse consciousness," *alayavijnana* in Sanskrit, *kun zhi nam shes* in Tibetan. The translation as storehouse has the connotation of being static, as if what it stores is preserved without change. I believe the translation as sub-stratum of awareness is more fitting as it suggests a more dynamic process. The sub-stratum of awareness itself goes through changes, so there is no concept that the unconscious stays the same, and that it is only the material within it that undergoes change. To reiterate, the sub-stratum of awareness is transformative and dynamic, as opposed to static or fixed.

Through sense perception and sense consciousness, we gain information about the outside world. This information is interpreted by the seventh consciousness, the egocentric mentation, in terms of self-referencing. This whole process leaves impressions on the unconscious where it remains in latent form as a potentiality that can be actualized if the appropriate circumstances arise. Therefore, we can be seen to act and respond to thoughts and circumstances in a particular way because of the latent karmic traces and dispositions, due to the interaction between the levels of consciousness.

There are not eight levels of consciousness as much as three levels of consciousness. The first is comprised of the five sense consciousnesses, and the sixth consciousness which gives order to what we experience through the senses; the second is the egocentric mentation, or self-centered perception; and the third is the substratum of awareness, the repository of all our latent traces and dispositions. Due to the interaction of these three levels, we apprehend and perceive the world dualistically. That is our normal experience. To transcend dualism, to transcend subject and object, we need to step out of our normal way of perceiving reality by tuning ourselves into the transcendental aspect in order to perceive reality as it is.

Four Levels of Consciousness in Dzogchen

In the Dzogchen tradition, four levels of the mind, or consciousness are presented.

The first level of mind in Dzogchen corresponds with the first level of consciousness of the Yogacara. That is, the five sense consciousnesses, and the sixth consciousness, which gives order to what we experience through the senses.

The second level of mind corresponds with the seventh level of consciousness of Yogacara—the egocentric mentation, which organizes our sensory input into categories or types, such as tables, chairs, people, et cetera.

The third level of mind corresponds with the eighth level of consciousness of Yogacara—the sub-stratum of awareness, where all the karmic traces and dispositions are deposited and past impressions are stored.

The fourth level of consciousness in the Dzogchen system is called *kun zhi* in Tibetan, the sub-stratum in Dzogchen. We find this fourth level of consciousness only in the Dzogchen tradition. This particular level of consciousness involves all the kinds of experiences that we have. Without the sub-stratum, then all the other levels of consciousness would not be able to exist due to the fact that the sub-stratum is seen as completely open and insubstantial. It is compared to the sky or space itself. It could be said the sub-stratum is the source of consciousness as such. Without space nothing could exist. There would be nothing whatsoever because there would be no space for anything to exist in. In a similar kind of way, without the sub-stratum there would be no such thing as experience of samsara, no such thing as experience of nirvana, no such thing as confusion, no such thing as enlightenment.

These four different levels of consciousness are not four different types that are completely disjointed and different, but rather it is the same consciousness with different levels of depth and clarity.

The reason one does Dzogchen practice is to be in more contact with our karmic reservoir, the storehouse consciousness, to see how we create karma, how our impressions get stored, and as a result, how our past impressions influence our way of thinking and perceiving. When we begin to realize and become aware of how that mechanism works, the more we are able to have some sense of, not necessarily control of, but at least an understanding of what is going on in our consciousness. Further, we start to realize, and come in contact with the sub-stratum, the source and the true condition that we are in, the authentic condition. So we can see the kun zhi, the sub-stratum, is our true nature.

Within this practice and approach, it is not suggested that our karmic impressions and emotional disturbances inhibit our ability to see the real nature of our mind. It does not mean that we should discard our karmic impressions and emotional disturbances, but simply acknowledge and become aware of them. Some kind of change of response is also necessary. For instance, if a pleasant experience arises, we may normally respond with happiness, and if an unnecessary or unwanted experience arises, our natural response may be anger and hostility.

Reversing one's normal response—if we have pleasant experiences, instead of responding to them with happiness, we can respond with hostility and see what happens in the mind. It is our tendency to respond in a certain way and normally act out of habit. Instead of doing the same thing again and again, if we respond differently, from an unconventional point of view, we begin to get another perspective on the same experience. What we call negativities are basically our interpretations. Further, due to our habitual response, we consolidate our attitudes and responses more, confounding situations and circumstances more and more. That is why in meditation, we should try to adopt the opposite attitude to help break the conventional notion of how one should react or not react.

Intensifying one's normal response—when we have an experience in meditation, in order to cut through karmic traces and dispositions and habitually entrenched ideas, whether it is joy, sadness, or any other experience, we can intensify it. If we feel joy, we generate more and more joy; we are bursting with joy. If we feel sad, then instead of thinking we shouldn't feel sad, or that we can't learn anything from sadness, instead, we intensify that experience until we can't bear it any more. By doing these types of intensifying practices, we can break certain barriers we have created and gain new insight. We have created so many limitations, mainly out of habit. These create barriers to experiencing more fully and directly. This provides another approach to addressing both our negativities and our positive experiences.

Our conventional attitudes are not predestined or static, we are perpetually constructing and re-constructing them. We can see notions of conventionality as just a convention. By giving ourselves the opportunity to give space to entrenched ideas, we find that conventions do not pre-exist without perpetually giving impetus for those behaviors to continue. If we stop perpetuating entrenched ideas, they begin to become more and more lucent. That is why we should develop a more relaxed attitude towards them. Otherwise, even meditation itself can become another habitual tendency and way of reacting to one's emotions, rather than a real technique for overcoming karmic habitual tendencies.

The Ordinary and the Transcendental

Dzogchenpas do not say that the world is made up just of the mind. Just because reality is not the way it appears does not mean that the consciousness has made it all up. How we experience the world is largely made up by the mind, but the world also has its own objectivity, which is not made up by our mind. Therefore, Dzogchenpas make a distinction between *nang wa* and *yul*. Nang wa means what we immediately perceive is constructed by the mind, but the object of appearance, yul, is not created by the mind. If everything were created by the mind, we find ourselves in an intellectual quagmire, because that suggests we would have created everyone we meet through our minds. For example, how I see you is constructed by me, but you are not made of my mind. Also, I may not have the ability to see you as you are, and that applies to whatever we experience be it trees, chairs, people, mountains, all experiences. The way we perceive may not be how it is.

By stepping out of our empirical perceptions of the world, when we get into the transcendental world we begin to see things differently, because we are not restricted by how things appear. We are able to go beyond the appearance and begin to see how things actually exist, how they really are. Appearance is different for every single person, but how things are is not different. A tree that exists by itself is the same, whether it appears to a Buddha or to a sentient being. However, the way it appears to those two individuals is different. A Buddha is able to see the tree as it exists whereas a sentient being is restricted to the way it appears. So we need to develop the ability to distinguish between how things are and how they appear.

This leads to a very interesting situation where through our transcendental consciousness we can understand that how things exist is the transcendental aspect of the world, the transcendental region of the world of the object. However, we cannot understand how things exist by using our ordinary consciousness. There is a real unity between the object and the subject in the transcendental aspect, whereas in the empirical experience of consciousness we are restricted by what we perceive. The empirical experience of the world is largely made up of our mind. What we perceive is restricted, and restriction comes about because of our own consciousness. All the materials that are drawn to construct this ordinary experience of the world, and about our self, is drawn from the unconscious.

Therefore, it is said that one should not mix the ordinary consciousness up with the transcendental consciousness because we can go astray and lose our sense of self. Dzogchenpas say that due to not being able to understand either the existence of the transcendental consciousness or the mistaken notion of identifying the two, not realizing the difference, we wander in the samsaric world. If we understand the transcendental aspect, then we begin to have the opportunity to self-actualize, to be able to realize oneself. Knowing oneself can take place only if we begin to look at ourselves and look at the existence of the transcendental aspect. Even if we just examine the ordinary consciousness and hope to gain some realization, Dzogchenpas say it is going to be very difficult. Self-realization does not come about from just understanding the workings of the ordinary consciousness. One has to understand the transcendental consciousness, and once one begins to understand that, then one begins to realize one is not as helpless and rigid as one normally thinks. We begin to realize that all our neurosis and all kinds of emotional afflictions come about because we have lost touch with the transcendental aspect.

The transcendental aspect is not embellished, contaminated, or polluted by our ordinary consciousness at all. From the transcendental aspect, no one can become insane, or neurotic, or psychotic, and once we begin to realize this, our obsession with the ordinary consciousness becomes attenuated, and we loosen our grip on it. The transcendental aspect then begins to reveal itself and we begin to gain real confidence about ourselves, which comes from transcending the ego. We can transcend the ego only if we can acknowledge the transcendental consciousness because the transcendental consciousness is all encompassing, whereas the ego is only a small thing that we tend to identify with. Identifying with the ordinary consciousness gives rise to ego, and ego gives rise to pride and arrogance, but it does not lead to confidence. Real self-confidence comes from the transcendental region. When we begin to realize we do not have to be arrogant or egocentric to function properly, we begin to trust ourselves and develop real appreciation of ourselves and we become less concerned or paranoid about our thoughts and behavior.

As long as we identify with our ordinary consciousness, there is paranoia. We are more afraid of ourselves than anything else. This fear leads to all kinds of mismanagement in terms of our relationships with others. The transcendental aspect helps us become more confident and we engender a very heroic approach, a warrior-like approach towards our emotions and neuroses, because they can be faced up to. Not only can we cope with them, but we can also manage and accommodate them, and give space for the emotions and neuroses to exist. It is our continuous struggle for space between us and the neurosis that has given rise to the neurosis in the first place. When we give some space to the neuroses, they become far less of an ordeal. One has a warrior-like approach by letting the neuroses be, rather than continuously fearing and struggling with them. Such struggles simply give rise to further neuroses.

If we begin to do that, we can begin to see people more directly, freer of the intentions to manipulate and exploit another. We often see others as objects because we are restricted to how the person appears to us. We cannot directly see the other person's consciousness visually, psychologically, or mentally, so we are restricted to seeing them based on how we apprehend their appearance and behavior. We cannot feel or experience whatever others are going through, although we might think we can. When we consider this, we realize our insight into another person is restricted by how they appear to us based on our own predetermined attitudes, perceptions, and so on. The transcendental concept allows us to go beyond that. Once we come into contact with aspects of our true nature, we are more in touch with ourselves, and then we can see other people's transcendental aspect as well. We begin to see others more fully as being human and less as objects. Interactions are no longer a relationship of "I" and "it." The relationship with the other person becomes more of an encounter.

We also see that freedom is intrinsic to transcendental consciousness, so to manipulate another person for our own gain is futile, because the other person possesses both consciousness and freedom. Therefore, the more we try to enslave or control another person, the more we become controlled. The western philosopher Hegel[13] noted this, saying that the master is as much enslaved by the slave as the slave is by the master. Without a slave there is no master. A master is so dependent upon the slave that the master is incapacitated without a slave. The slave is not completely enslaved as they have the capacity not to be used as an object. It is obvious, but normally we forget that we cannot control another human being. We believe in that attitude, but there is no such thing as controlling another human being because freedom, in the broad sense of just being able to be free, is intrinsic to every single person.

There are two notions of freedom—freedom to be and freedom to act. Freedom to act may be restricted due to circumstance and other inhibiting factors, but freedom to be has no limit, as it is intrinsic to the transcendental consciousness. Such unlimited freedom engenders compassionate and loving responsiveness where we have more resonance with everything. We resonate with other human beings, other sentient beings, and with whatever surrounds us. There is a real sense of a direct vibrational connection taking place where compassion is no longer based on sentimentality, and love is no longer based on attachment. Much of the time, contrary to our best efforts, we realize our compassionate acts are driven by sentimentality of some kind, taking pity on someone, or that they can even be used as a tool of manipulation.

Due to the sense of freedom to be, some kind of resonance takes place. Compassion, or responsiveness, is called *thug je* in Tibetan, which has the connotation of resonating. It is said that an enlightened person's compassion is like that of the sun reflected in water. The water resonates with the sun—it does not have any concepts, it does not intellectualize or rationalize. It is very natural for the water to reflect the sun. Similarly, our compassion becomes a natural response to the situation, rather than something that we do. When we get into the transcendental aspect, compassion has nothing to do with doing things. That is how the Dzogchenpas understand the relationship between our ordinary experience and transcendental experience. We cannot do away with the ordinary consciousness, but we have to acknowledge the existence of the transcendental region in order to understand the way in which the two operate. There is a real sense of interaction and interdependence between the two.

Three Orders of Reality

The notion of the three orders of reality was also introduced by the Yogacarans.

The first order or reality is "the ground of being," or "ideally absolute," *parinispanna* in Sanskrit, *yong drub* in Tibetan. The second order is called "causal relationship," or "relative," *paratantra* in Sanskrit, *zhan wang* in Tibetan. The third order is "conceptual apparatus," or "notional-conceptual," *parikalpita* in Sanskrit, *kun tags* in Tibetan.

The ground of being refers to the way in which things actually exist, or the reality of things. The meaning of the terms rigpa and emptiness, for instance, would constitute what is known as the ground of being, where there is no differentiation between subject and object. The first order is sometimes translated as "ideally absolute." "Absolute" can often refer to a god or underlying reality, however, that is not the meaning here. Absolute in this context means that the ground of being is already present within the relative.

The second order is based upon causal relationships, and that is how things exist in the relative sense. Whatever we perceive, and whatever we experience, even psychologically and internally, there is nothing that has come about without being dependent upon causes and conditions. That is why it is called "causal relationship," or "relative."

The conceptual apparatus, the third order, refers to our use of concepts in relation the second order of reality, causal relationships. The third order is our conceptual representation of the second order. So the third order is an interpretation of how we see causal relationships, how things exist in the relative sense. For example, when we look at the tree, we don't see that particular tree, how it has come about due to soil, rain, sunshine, and all the other conditions that are necessary for it to exist. Rather, we see the picture of the tree using our conceptual frame of reference, parikalpita or conceptual apparatus. We do not see the tree as it is. How the tree exists has nothing to do with our mental picture of the tree, but we do not experience it that way. We only see the picture of that particular tree in association with the kind of general mental picture we have of what are called "trees." We are using the conceptual frame of reference with the second order of reality.

This particular concept is formed due to the principle of what is called *zhan sel* in Tibetan. Zhan sel means something like "principle of exclusion," excluding what is not relevant and only concentrating on what is relevant. Whenever we see a tree we say, "The tree is not a stone, it's not a house, it's not this, it's not that." So we conclude that it is a tree. Whenever we see something, it is always based upon the principle zhan sel—it's not this, it's not that, therefore it is this.

Our way of thinking is representational, picture-like. Therefore, we do not see things directly. We always see things as being this, as being that, rather than seeing things, whatever object of perception it may be, in that particular mode, in a very direct sense, as how it exists.

The notional-conceptual, or the conceptual apparatus, is also being used in relation to our belief systems. Belief systems are interpretations of what we have empirically observed and based on those observations we build up all kinds of interpretations— different philosophies, different views, different religions. That is all considered to be based upon the third principle, or the third order of reality, the notional-conceptual.

In the Dzogchen tradition, we seek to overcome our obsessive concern with the conceptual apparatus in order to see each individual thing as it is, as it stands, in relation to the relative. We begin to see that because it is relative, it is founded upon something. If it were not relative, it would not have to depend upon anything else. Everything that exists is dependent upon something else, which is emptiness in the objective sense, and rigpa in the subjective sense, the unity of which constitutes the ground of being.

Chapter Four

Self-Existing Wisdom

The Ground of Being

As mentioned previously, it is necessary to distinguish between the ordinary consciousness and the transcendental consciousness. Self-existing wisdom, or the ground of being, refers to the original natural state of the mind or the transcendental consciousness. It serves as the backdrop for all of our experiences of samsara and nirvana, and is also the basis of sustaining our abilities to develop wisdom and our ability to eradicate ignorance and confusion. Without the ground of being, nothing would be possible. The ground of being is the pre-condition that makes everything possible. There are several terms in Dzogchen which refer to the original, natural state of the mind—"self-existing wisdom," *rang jung yeshe* in Tibetan; "mind in itself," *sems nyid*; "ground of being," *zhi*; and sometimes it is also called the "King of Self-Creation," *kungzhi gyalpo*. The ground of being, our natural state, has been pure right from the beginning, it is the alpha state, the primordial state. The ground of being has never been corrupted or vitiated by our defilements or obscurations, which are the product of primordial ignorance.

Primordial Purity

Primordial purity is called *ka dag* in Tibetan. *Ka* is the first word in the Tibetan alphabet, so that symbolizes "the beginning," and *dag* means "pure." So ka dag means "alpha pure" or "primordial purity," right from the beginning. This suggests, no matter how corrupted, depressed, or terrible we feel, right from the beginning, we have been endowed with this incorruptible primordial purity, which neither increases nor decreases. That is to say, if we are drifting in the samsaric condition, it is not diminished, and if we become enlightened, it is not increased. It is the basic primordial purity.

Spontaneous establishment

Spontaneous establishment, *lhundrub* in Tibetan, has two aspects. The first, the spontaneous establishment of the phenomenal world, *chergyen lhundrub* in Tibetan, means that every single thing, entity, or experience we have day-to-day, is spontaneously perfected. Everything is unique and perfect within itself. Every experience that we have, of happiness, unhappiness, and all variations of our experiences are spontaneously established in the context of samsara and nirvana. Every single thing or entity that we encounter in the world, is spontaneously established within the three times of past, present, and future. Every single thing that we encounter in the world is spontaneously established in respect to dharmadhatu, or reality itself.

As it has been said,

> "When things manifest, when each single thing manifests by itself, singularly, then that thing is spontaneously established and is perfect in its own right. So in that way, whatever manifests is already established in the reality itself."

The second spontaneous establishment is the reality aspect. Reality, even though it does not have any characteristics or attributes of its own, nonetheless, it is spontaneously established in the phenomena that manifest, that are perceptible, that have attributes, and so on.

As this particular quotation says,

> "The *dharmadatu*, or the reality, is present in things that have attributes, and therefore the phenomenal world is more important than the reality, because it is through the phenomenal world that the unconditioned nature of the reality is revealed."

Essence, Nature, and Energy

The three elements of essence, nature, and energy, are the aspects of the ground of being, how things actually are, or how things exist.

Unlike the metaphysical concept of essences, which are supposed to reside in the inner core of things, essence in this particular context, is understood as emptiness, meaning there is nothing that is absolute. Whatever we experience from the external world is relative, as nothing remains unchanged or persists forever. If we turn our attention within ourselves, that is also what we find. Within or without, everything is relative and therefore empty. Emptiness can be misunderstood as something different from what we normally experience. However, emptiness refers to nothing other than the relativity of things, because things are dependent upon one another, and are thus interdependent, as Nagarjuna has expounded in relation to *pratityasamutpada*, interdependent origination.[14]

Nature is related with the fact that because things are empty, because things are dependent upon each other, then things never come to cease. This process continues because things are dynamic, and continues to cause things to manifest. In the Dzogchen context, when we meditate and develop an understanding of the idea of emptiness, that does not mean we stop using concepts. Rather, because we understand our mental events—concepts, ideas, thoughts, and so forth are not real or substantial within themselves, we have further impetus to use our thoughts, ideas, and concepts incessantly and to our advantage.

Energy refers to the potency of the dynamic experience, that whatever experiences we might be having are in a dynamic process and that is totally potent. There is a lot of potency in terms of our experience of the whole thing.

Energy is unceasing in terms of its process. The reason why there is energy in the first place is because the whole idea of static-ness is not present. Energy has three aspects, which are known as *tsal, dang*, and *rolpa* in Tibetan. These three words are very hard to translate, but we can get an approximate idea if we translate tsal as dexterity, dang as transparency, and rolpa as sensation.

Tsal, or dexterity, implies that even when our mind is in a state of disarray and confusion, nonetheless, it is unceasingly energetic and always in a process. Also, the mind is so skillful in terms of its manifestations even if it is manifesting in terms of anger, jealousy, pride, or whatever. The way in which the mind can manifest in different ways is so dexterous there is no limit to the kind of things that the mind can come up with. Therefore, it is considered to be an enormous source of energy and potentiality. This is due to the mind's limitless capabilities that can be contrasted with our physical condition.

The second aspect, dang, or transparency, means that even when our mind is in a state of confusion, it is never opaque or solid. Even when we are subjected to confusion, indecisiveness, and so forth, or even in a state of extraordinary emotional upheaval, our mind is always transparent. The mind is never hidden from itself, it is always transparent, thus is free from opaqueness.

The third aspect, rolpa, refers to the mind's ability to experience varieties of sensations through the medium of the body. When we come in contact with any external objects, the mind is able to experience varieties of sensations. Rolpa also has the connotation of enjoyment.

Those are the three aspects of energy in relation to the unceasing manifestations of the mind. This tripartite is something that is neither rejected nor cultivated, but is simply seen as different aspects of the mind. The mind is like a crystal that can assume varieties of colors because of the external conditions. So the mind, basic awareness, as it manifests as a process, can assume various kinds of appearance, but mind itself has no particular characteristics.

Meditation

Before beginning the visualization, settle into meditation posture, rest the mind for a few minutes, letting the mind settle naturally while being aware of the breath.

With this particular practice we visualize a crystal as the heart centre, and the varieties of the experiences that we have in terms of emotions, thoughts, and so forth, as lights and colours bouncing off the crystal. The crystal symbolizes bare awareness, or rigpa, and the lights and colours bouncing off it symbolize the varieties of emotional energies that manifest in terms of those three aspects of energy—tsal, dang, and rolpa. Those three aspects of energy, thug je, accompany all our mental processes.

After spending some time with the visualization, dissolve it, and let the mind rest naturally.

Six Misinterpretations of the Ground of Being

Self-existing wisdom, the ground of being, can be easily misunderstood. When one contemplates the ground of being, certain misunderstandings may arise, and therefore certain warnings are given in regard to this. Traditionally, six different kinds of misinterpretations are presented.

First, if one believes the ground of being is spontaneously

established, then one could believe both our confusions and our wisdom are spontaneously established right from the beginning. If it is understood in that way, it becomes difficult to embark on the path, and liberation becomes difficult if ignorance is already entrenched within the notion of self-establishment, or spontaneous establishment.

Second, we could mistakenly see the ground of being as something that is indeterminate in itself. It would be something that would change, and something that can be organized and shaped by our attitudes. If that were so, the ground of being would cease to be something that is real, it would become relative to our needs and desires, and in fact could become subjected to our confused ideas and confusions.

The third means that the ground of being is completely unchanging. If it is unchanging, then it becomes difficult to conceive how one could become enlightened. If the ground of being is seen as something that is totally unchanging, then the idea of enlightenment becomes difficult to conceive.

The fourth means that the ground of being can be changed, and if one believes this to be so, even if one has attained the spiritual state of the fruition stage, one can still regress.

The fifth is connected with the extreme views of seeing the ground of being as either eternal or impermanent. If one sees the ground of being in such a manner, then it becomes subjected to the two extreme wrong views of eternalism and nihilism.

The sixth is the view that whatever arises in our mind is the ground of being itself, in which case the ground of being becomes relativized and becomes impermanent. Therefore, the ground of being has to be understood as being difficult to understand and difficult to articulate. If we were to engage in these things with respect to the ground of being, then it would be very difficult.

If we understand the ground of being as pure from the

beginning, not existing as an entity, then we can avoid the extreme of eternalism. The ground of being is also manifest in the relative or phenomenal world, and because it is spontaneously established within the relative or phenomenal world, it does not fall into the nihilistic extreme either. Therefore, the ground of being avoids the two extremes of eternalism and nihilism.

So, on the one hand the ground of being does not have any attributes or characteristics, unlike entities we encounter in the phenomenal world. On the other hand, it manifests in the relative world as inherent in the things and entities that we encounter in everyday life.

Another important point is that as the ground of being is pure from the beginning, one could mistakenly believe there is no need for meditation practice. If it is pure right from the beginning, for all intents and purposes, one is already enlightened. Even though the ground of being itself is pure, nonetheless there are adventitious defilements that we need to purify. Those defilements should be seen as dreamlike, not as being substantial and real. So, from this perspective, the ground of being can be seen as obscured by temporary defilements, which can be removed. Therefore, there is no contradiction in seeing the ground of being as primordially pure and, at the same time realizing there are defilements that need to be removed.

The ground of being is itself completely unconditioned and it can never be conditioned. No one has the ability to condition it, not even a Buddha. It is also spontaneously present, and therefore it cannot be brought into existence. The ground of being is also the foundation, the ground of all existence. Without it then there would be nothing in existence, because everything is ontologically dependent on it.

All other yanas, except for the Dzogchen teachings, entertain the idea that the phenomenal world is ultimately unreal and it is something that needs to be transcended. However, from the Dzogchen point of view, we cannot transcend the phenomenal world because reality and the phenomenal world are intimately bound together. There is no rupture between reality and appearance, or the phenomenal world.

Therefore, we cannot say that when we are confused we are perceiving only the phenomenal world, and when we become enlightened, we then perceive dharmadatu, or the all-encompassingness of reality, emptiness. With such a conception, those two perceptions of the world would cancel each other out— when the phenomenal world is present, then reality is not present, it is hidden by the appearance, and when reality is present, then the phenomenal world is not present, it has become illusory, so it is something that needs to be transcended.

With such a view, we create an enormous chasm between the two domains of the world. If there is a rupture between our immediate phenomenal word, and reality or emptiness, then the whole idea of enlightenment would become impossible. Because no matter how hard we tried to develop spiritually—engaging in meditation, trying to transform the mind, trying to develop a more enlightened attitude—all these things take place in the relative world. It is then difficult to explain how by working with the phenomenal world one would be able to understand reality, which is considered to be something completely different to the world that we have immediate contact with.

Finally, as the ground of being is present in everyone, without any distinction, and is pure, how is it that some people are spiritually predisposed and progress quickly on the path, while others remain the same or even regress? The ground of being itself does not change, it is primordially pure and ever-present. However, our ordinary mind has varying degrees of sensitivity regarding matters of spirituality. It is the ordinary mind that has to be distinguished from the ground of being, or self-existing wisdom. Therefore, it is only due to our subjective mind and judgments of ourselves and others that we can make distinctions between people who are developed, those who are less so, and those yet to embark on a spiritual path. If we believe there is a distinction or fundamental difference in the ground of being itself between individuals, then the ground of being would cease to be considered ultimate and would become relative. Also, the ground of being itself could be judged to be more sublime in respect to some individuals and profane in respect to some other individuals. That, however, is not the case.

Going Astray

Since one has not been able to recognize primordial purity, one goes astray, or wanders away, *trulpa* in Tibetan. What we are wandering away from is the transcendental self, our natural condition, we are not wandering away from anything else. That is due to varieties of confusions that have been generated as a result of primordial ignorance, which is sustained through the interaction with the different levels of consciousness. We interact with the external world through the five senses. Information is gathered via the five senses and is filtered through our consciousness, and is then processed by the egocentric mentation. Eventually all this material is stored in the sub-stratum of awareness, the unconscious. These impressions, known as bag chags in Tibetan, *vasanas* in Sanskrit, are referred to as karmic traces and dispositions. Because of these karmic traces and dispositions, one gets into the habit of behaving in a particular way and that would then generate further traces and dispositions. This leads to our becoming caught up in what is known as "cyclic existence," samsara.

Once we begin to realize we have gone astray from our natural condition, we begin to understand ourselves more. Dzogchen has got nothing to do with understanding the world, or reality as it exists outside. We cannot start examining the reality outside. Dzogchen practice starts from inside, from one's own transcendental side and expands outwards from there. One tries to understand the transcendental aspect of the world, but one does not try to discover the reality of things and ignore the transcendental consciousness. The starting point is oneself, self-actualization, and being oneself in an authentic sense. Not conditioning ourselves, not trying to be this or that. That is the problem of ordinary consciousness, always wanting to do this or that, or adopt this or that particular identity, or this or that self-image. The transcendental has none of that—one just is, one has just to let oneself be.

We don't discover the transcendental region, as much as the transcendental region reveals itself to us. We need to let it reveal itself rather than try to discover it. If we try to discover the transcendental region, then we are attempting to condition it, and therefore we are not letting ourselves rest in the natural state. Therefore, it has been said that we cannot look for, seek, or discover the transcendental region; rather, we have to let ourselves be so the transcendental region reveals itself.

A person who is able to rest in their authentic condition is an individual who has been able to thoroughly work with their relationship towards their ego, and also, has exhausted all the karmic seeds that are sowed in the sub-stratum of awareness, the level of consciousness in which all our karmic and habitual traces and dispositions are stored. When someone realizes their authentic condition, they are able to exhaust all karmic traces and be in their natural state. As a result of that, one's knowledge regarding oneself and one's true condition is revealed. Therefore, the person begins to realize that what we call "ego" is a convenient device that one has created, and is continuously creating, as a reference point in relation to oneself and the external world. However, this ego is not an independent entity, or something that is lasting and unchanging, but something in continuous process, and one begins to realize the ego is really insubstantial.

Chapter Five

Self-Liberation and how Confusion Arises

Having looked at the idea of self-existing wisdom, the ground of being upon which all samsaric and nirvanic experiences ultimately rest, we will now look into how we become confused and lose touch with our fundamental existential condition.

In Dzogchen and other Buddhist approaches, it is ignorance that has caused this confusion, and it is ignorance that contributes to perpetuating our samsaric condition. Ignorance is understood differently within the different Buddhist perspectives. From the Hinayana perspective, ignorance is the state of mind where one mistakenly believes that what is impure is pure, what is suffering is blissful, what is impermanent is permanent, and that the non-substantial ego is permanent and self-existing. From the Mahayana perspective, ignorance is understood in relation to the two levels of truth, absolute truth and relative truth. Ignorance is seen as an innate tendency within us to think that everything exists substantially and permanently. Therefore, ignorance lies in not being able to make the distinction between relative truth and absolute truth. In the Vajrayana or Tantra, ignorance is seen as not being able to see one's divine nature, which is dormant. From the Dzogchen point of view, ignorance is tied up with the understanding that right from the beginning, one's existential condition has never been corrupted by confusion, such as excessive desires and perpetuating diminishing behaviors and attitudes.

Three Modes of Confusion

The first mode of confusion is "the basis of our confusion is the ground of being itself," *rigpa senjur tulpa yeshe* in Tibetan. There is no other basis for the origin of our confusion than within the ground of being, which is perceived to be uncorrupted. The cause of the confusion is ignorance. No specific date can be assigned to when confusion began. Confusion is present in the ground of being because of ignorance, and it is beginningless.

The nature of the confusion is the tendency to grasp on to one's selfhood. The mode of the confusion derives from seeing the mind in itself, the true nature of the mind which is unitary, as a duality. Because of this, we develop varieties of dualistic thoughts and notions that generate further confusion. This process of generation perpetuates our samsaric condition as we assume different modes of existence. The traditional example of our perpetuating the samsaric condition is of a spider that spins a web and then gets caught in it and chokes itself to death.

As a particular text states:

"From the ground of being, our existential condition, arises all the confusions which are related with conceptual proliferations, and from that comes attachment, possessiveness, and that generates suffering, unhappiness, and so on. This intensifies due to our attitude of saying, 'This is mine, this belongs to me.'"

Ultimately, no one binds us to the samsaric condition and there is no one who has condemned us to this state except our own mistaken concepts and ideas. There is no one who is responsible for our confused state. It is due to our own mistaken concepts and ideas that we have ended up this way.

The second mode of becoming confused is "the confusion generated in relation to the five lights," *wernung widgya turje* in

Tibetan. The existential mode of self-existing wisdom is totally luminous and radiates five different lights. When these five different lights are not understood properly, then one's awareness becomes lessened, decreased, and dimmed. By not realizing that the five different lights actually originate from the self-existing wisdom, the ground of being, then one has generated dualistic notions, and with that comes co-emergent ignorance. The reason why it is called co-emergent ignorance is because ignorance manifests simultaneously with wisdom. Ignorance in this context has to do with not realizing the simultaneous manifestation of wisdom and ignorance.

The third one is called "the way in which one becomes confused in relation to emptiness, reality, or encompassingness." The five different types of lights, which are related with self-existing wisdom, are connected with the five elements. For instance, the wisdom that manifests as a light in relation to mirror-like wisdom has the water element corresponding to that, and the color is white. The light radiating in relation to the wisdom of equanimity has the earth element corresponding to that, and the color is yellow. The light radiating in conjunction with the wisdom of discrimination has the fire element corresponding to it, and the color is red. The light radiating in conjunction with the wisdom of accomplishment has the wind element corresponding to it, and the color is green. The light radiating from the self-existing wisdom signifies the space element which is dark blue in color.

These are also related with what are often referred to as the five poisons, the five primary negative emotional states. The earth element relates to pride, the water element relates to anger, the fire element to desire, the wind element to jealousy, and the space element to ignorance. In conjunction with all this, from the Dzogchen point of view comes the confused state. Once we have a degree of understanding of how the process of confusion works, then the idea is not to try to get rid of, or try to overcome the so-called poisons, but rather, we see the poisons for what they are and also recognize that there is a wisdom component corresponding to all the elements and the poisons. The mistake, or the ignorance, lies in not being able to understand this, rather than there being something substantial or real to be discarded or overcome.

For this reason, in Dzogchen, it is said that there is nothing to be accepted and nothing to be rejected, because realizing the nature of samsara is to realize the true condition of things. If samsara is rejected and discarded, then there is nothing to be realized. Therefore, in Dzogchen we develop the attitude of neither accepting nor rejecting. One does not try to cultivate things that are conducive towards attaining enlightenment, nor does one try to reject and discard things belonging to the samsaric condition. If one is able to develop awareness and not fall into these two extremes, then one will be able to understand the true existential condition of things in their proper mode. It has also been said that by letting the phenomenal world be as it is, instead of trying to change it, does not mean that one would become more confused. By letting it remain as it is, then one becomes released, because it is not the phenomenal world which binds us, but the attachment and aversions that we have within ourselves towards how we experience the phenomenal world. That is the principal reason why we are bound to the samsaric condition in the first place.

The Dzogchen view is that everything that we experience in relation to ourselves and the world is dynamic. Nothing is static, including human nature. According to Dzogchen, there is no such thing as fixed human nature, because if everything is in a process, then we cannot sustain a view of human nature that persists through different eras and cultural, social, and biological changes. Therefore, we cannot say that human nature is fixed or completely conditioned by external influences such as the society.

Human nature is often used by philosophers and others to justify different types of behaviors, such as oppression. For example, the idea of human nature has been used in order to place women in subordinate roles, to promote racism, and so forth. All different kinds of theories of human nature have been put forward over time, however none are absolute in themselves. In fact, no one has yet put forward a comprehensive theory of human nature. Basically, what it boils down to is that everyone is in a state of process and never in a fixed position. This is where the idea of self-liberation, *rang drol* in Tibetan, comes in.

There are five different kinds of self-liberation that have been formulated in the Dzogchen system.

The first one is *ye drol* in Tibetan, meaning that the individual has been freed right from the beginning, inferring that the freedom one achieves is not introduced to the person via external circumstances, thus the person is intrinsically free. Ye means primordially, and drol means to be liberated, to be free. Therefore, the freedom is not achieved because of some external change of circumstance, but rather, it is intrinsic to the make-up of the individual.

The second one is rang drol in Tibetan, meaning self-liberation. Rang drol here means that our passions, emotions, and so on become self-liberated. We do not have to use antidotes in order to control our passions and emotions. We do not have to try to control our anger, jealousy, envy, or pride, because by their own nature, the passions are self-liberated. In terms of meditation practice, one simply becomes aware of the varieties of experiences that they have. Instead of trying to use some antidote, as one would normally do in other forms of meditation, one just simply lets the experience be so that the experience becomes self-liberated.

The third one is *cer drol* in Tibetan. *Cer* means naked, and *drol* means to become liberated again. When we perceive something, we can just simply observe and remain with the object without adding interpretations, conceptual categorization, and value judgments. That is why it is called "naked"—naked of all our conceptual proliferation, one is completely in tune with the pure presence of the whole object. In Dzogchen practice this is even done deliberately and consciously.

The fourth one is *tha drol* in Tibetan. Tha drol means one is liberated, as one is no longer confined by labels and extreme views. When one is experiencing anything, the experiences are not labeled as being good or bad, positive or negative, et cetera. *Tha* means extreme, and *drol* is to be liberated. Thus tha drol means liberation from extreme views and dogmatism, excessive attachment to words, language, and concepts and so forth.

The fifth one, which is known as *cig drol,* is the most important in this particular system. Cig drol means "liberation of one," which refers to rigpa, or basic awareness. In the Dzogchen teachings, the reason we avoid putting value-judgments and interpretations on our experience is in order to let our own basic awareness, our rigpa arise. So cig drol means that as soon as our basic awareness arises, we are freed from all the other bondages that we have created. Basic awareness manifests not when a person is engaged in interpreting one's experiences as being spiritual or not spiritual, et cetera, but when the person begins to suspend their judgment about their own experience. Then the possibility of rigpa, or basic awareness arising is much more enhanced.

That is why it is said in Dzogchen that strictly following certain procedures, rules, and regulations is not necessary. If our life and conduct becomes too regulated, then the possibility of spontaneity and creativity, and the manifestation of basic awareness, becomes less available. That is why being in the natural state is encouraged, that is, to remain with whatever one is experiencing, whether uplifted or solemn. Rather than trying to change or fight an experience, one simply tries to remain aware of it.

View, Meditation, and Action

There are many different philosophical views presented within the various Buddhist traditions. In any Buddhist school, view, meditation, and action are very important. That is because there is a particular philosophical view presented, there is a description on how that philosophical view could be meditated on and looked at from the experiential point of view, and there is the experience having effect on how we act. We can often forget the inter-relationship between view, meditation, and action, and are not as aware of the relationship between these three as we should be. In Buddhism, when following a particular view, we need to understand the view intellectually through study and debate, meditate to gain realization of the view from an experiential perspective, and then that experience should be translated into action. It is not the point to philosophize for the sake of philosophizing. Further, our meditation practice can lack clarity and direction if we are without a solid philosophical understanding of the view being presented.

Some practitioners may meditate without a proper grounding in the philosophical context, while others may philosophize but do not meditate, and assume things will eventually become clear through intellectual investigation alone. However, from the Buddhist point of view, these three basic principles of view, meditation, and action are all essential and must be interrelated.

The view from the Dzogchen perspective is slightly different from other Buddhist schools as the Dzogchen view is of no view; it is a trans-view. It is not another philosophical view. It is a view that allows a person to be free from all kinds of fixations and views. Dzogchenpas say that we should not be biased by what we believe. We may believe in Buddhist philosophy and believe that these views are more worthwhile than others, however, we have to acknowledge that it is just a belief and nothing more.

If it is an incorrigible law that has been passed down to us and somehow controls our life, it will only serve us for practical purposes. One should not let oneself become dogmatic and rigid and have a straight-jacket approach to life because of Buddhist views. We should not play one's views against others or develop prejudices towards others who do not share our viewpoints. Conflicts do not necessarily occur because of how people treat us, or how they think of us. Conflict is more likely to arise because of differing views on the state of the world, politics, and religion. Holding rigid views makes communication between people difficult. Like anyone else, if Buddhists develop a rigid viewpoint, it leads to conflict and breakdown in communication.

The Dzogchen perspective has an aerial point of view that looks at the human condition objectively, from the summit, with a non-biased attitude. As a Dzogchen practitioner, one should have respect towards all the other schools of Buddhism, and to the innumerable views presented. One should not arrogantly purport the Dzogchen view to be the best, or as one's saving grace. If looked at from that viewpoint, then the particular expansive view that is being presented is narrowed down immediately, and what we are doing is presenting another philosophical viewpoint. That is why it is said that the Dzogchen view is the view of no view. It is the view that overcomes all views—overcomes all biases, prejudices, and dogmatism of all kinds, not holding onto concepts rigidly, making them concrete, and consolidating them.

That leads to one no longer viewing samsara as being a terrible place where people suffer and experience confinement and bondage, and nirvana is no longer viewed as freedom where people experience happiness. Those two attitudes are also overcome. By incorporating those different attitudes towards samsara and nirvana, one begins to have a very expansive outlook.

Meditation is related with not getting distracted, and not

becoming vulnerable and getting subjected to the states of mind of depression and elation.[15] Other than that, whatever we experience is part of meditation. In Dzogchen, one does not need to experience calmness of the mind to be in meditation. Whether one's mind is disturbed or at ease, both of these states of mind are part of the meditative experience. If one is feeling agitated while meditating, that should not be seen as anathema to meditation or as cancelling out the calm state of mind we may have developed. Agitation should not be regarded as regression, but rather as part of the process itself. In Dzogchen, meditation is practiced in order to bring forward what is latent or hidden in our subconscious or unconscious. Instead of using meditation as a technique of repressing and consolidating our resistance, we use meditation in order to bring out what is already there. If we are feeling agitation, experiencing anger, jealousy, pride, and numerous other experiences associated with those mental states, we do not see those states as being suddenly brought about by meditation.

It is not that we have been so unemotional in the past that when we start practicing Dzogchen meditation, we are suddenly faced with dramatic emotions. The meditation allows us to see what we may not have been aware of so explicitly before. It brings forward to our attention what is latently already there. These emotions and disturbances invariably affect the way we see things, how we act, and interact with others. All the disturbances, prejudices, and attitudes have a direct or indirect effect on our lives. It is better to look at what arises in the mind and not turn away. To confront what arises in the mind openly is a more heroic approach. That is, to allow what arises to be there. This approach is anathema to weaknesses derived from retreating or judging when neurosis and negativities manifest in meditation. Turning away can lead to a lack of trust and belief about oneself and others. Being able to relate to others is difficult if we are not willing to relate to ourselves. If there is a conflict relating to oneself, then it is likely a problem relating to others as well. This is why it can be very difficult to overcome the notion of subject and object.

The whole thrust or orientation of Dzogchen practice is to overcome our ordinary conventional dualistic notion of subject and object. This comes about through successful communication and interaction with other human beings, which develops through loving kindness, compassion, and having a proper view. The meditative state is seen as being free from distraction. That is the definition of Dzogchen meditation. As long as one is not distracted by depression and elation, as long as one's rigpa is operating and one is just right there in the presence of one's emotional states, then one is in a meditative state. One does not have to worry about what is going on from a psychological perspective. If the mind is in a dramatic state with much activity, that is all well and good. The mental events and activities need to be assimilated rather than pushed aside, judged, or proliferated.

When one starts to practice meditation, one begins to reassess one's situation, as well as reassess one's perception of the world. From that comes the action, the actual application of what one has learned in terms of philosophy, one's worldview, and one's meditative experiences. Until then, one cannot be authoritative in terms of usefulness or potency of one's actions. A lot of the time, we can only rely on customs, rules, and so forth in order to act in the right or appropriate manner. When ruled by our prejudices, we cannot trust our judgments or our understanding of the situation completely. We can be limited to following prescribed social and customary rules of engagement.

Through meditation, one can establish a more open and realistic worldview. Then one is in a better position to apply that in daily life. One is able to transcend the belief in the fixed nature of rules and customs and be less bound by them. This includes Buddhist ethics as it is set forward in the vinaya[16] sutras. It is easy to think that ethical codes, for example, as those presented in the vinaya sutras, are something absolute. In fact, there is nothing absolute in that at all. All moral rules and regulations are relative.

On the other hand, that does not mean that one can do whatever one feels like. That is absolutely not the point at all. The point is to be able to respect the conventional mode of behavior, mode of ethics, and the conventional mode of morality, without having to think that these value systems are absolute and fixed. We can have a more liberal and open-minded attitude towards these things, but that should not lead us to an amoral avenue of life.

The reason why actions should not be completely bound by rules and regulations is because sometimes rules and regulations correspond with how things actually are, and other times rules and regulations do not correspond with how things actually are. If one were completely bound by moral rules, sometimes one would not be able to do a beneficial act in case that upset certain rules and regulations.

It is important to learn how to be spontaneous and react to individual situations effectively, and not be bound by certain rigid codes of morality, to then fail to respond to a situation directly and effectively. In Dzogchen, the spontaneity aspect in one's action is encouraged so that one is not bound by past experiences and future expectations. The person acts because that response is required in given situations to be of the greatest benefit. The person is not acting because of some compulsion or habit, or past experiences or impressions. Nor is that person's way of behaving drawn towards future obsessions, thus losing perspective on the circumstances as they present themselves in the current situation. One's actions can be ineffective or backfire if driven solely by inculcated influences.

What is being said here is that our technical knowledge about how we should be behaving and how we should be doing things can also include creativity in how we operate and respond. In Dzogchen, the way we take action is to take into account contingencies and always look for the unexpected. The unexpected is always included in what is happening. In terms of how we go about acting upon and addressing the circumstances we find ourselves in, we cannot have total faith in prescriptions and in all kinds of technical methods.

It is said that one's action should be effortless, *tsol med* in Tibetan. What that means is that we always allow for some spaciousness within our efforts. Sometimes when we do things, we want to do them properly and precisely and we demand a lot of ourselves. If we want something to be perfect, we may try too hard and this can backfire on us. Effortless action does not mean sitting around. That would not be action. Effortless action, or the Zen or Taoist term "action of non-action," is not about cruising around on the beach barefoot or something. Effortlessness refers to always reminding ourselves of our transcendental aspect, by allowing some sense of spaciousness within our endeavors.

If we have a sense of relaxation within our endeavors, we are able to see things more clearly and begin to see what action is required. However, if we are trying too hard, our focus can become narrowed and distorted, and it is easy to become all worked up in this state. We can lose perspective and invariably will make poor decisions and even lose faith in whatever we are doing. Even if working on an extremely valuable project, a commendable task, our approach may be what leads to a sense of failure. One may regret ever beginning such a task, and doubt the worthiness of the endeavor in the first place, or possibly seeing the cause as entirely external.

Effortlessness is regarded as extremely important. One is encouraged to always approach one's life from the perspective of effortlessness—to avoid trying too hard, and avoiding getting too worked up. This is common sense but a lot of the time that is not how we operate. That is why we need to be reminded.

Three Types of Action

As the practitioner begins to realize the Dzogchen view, gains experience in meditation, and receives guidance from accomplished Dzogchen practitioners, one's actions are intrinsically affected in three ways.

The first is called "secret action," *sang chod* in Tibetan. *Sang* means secret, and *chod* means action. For this practitioner, no matter what their actions are, their rigpa is present and they can act with certainty. There is no doubt about their motives as they understand their own mind so much that there is no way they could do something that is of no benefit to themselves or others. Whether one is walking, sitting, or sleeping, it becomes part of the meditation and part of further growth. No matter what they do, any action they initiate is going to be self-liberated. The traditional analogy is of precipitation of snow on a boulder. When the snow hits the boulder, it precipitates, no damage is being done. In a similar way, whatever action the person at this level engages in does not impact their mind or leave karmic impressions. It simply dissipates by itself. Therefore, the person can respond spontaneously in a variety of ways and remain in the state of rigpa.

The second is called "actualization of rigpa," *rigpa tulshug* in Tibetan, and is a deeper level of secret action. Not only is their behavior unconventional privately, but their behavior can also manifest unconventionally in public. Rigpa is present in their actions and will benefit themselves and others due to their pure motivation and perception. The person may do things that would astound other people. If we look at Indian history, a lot of siddhas engaged in unconventional activities. Sometimes their behavior was shocking and sometimes they got into trouble.

The third is known as "communal participation," *tsog chod* in Tibetan. Communal participation means that the practitioner of

Dzogchen can go into any community, or a crowd of people, and no matter what is going on, they are able to maintain rigpa, and their behavior does not get out of hand. Even when their behavior is unconventional, they maintain rigpa and are fully aware. Their actions are not disruptive or insane but performed with total awareness.

It is prohibited for monastics—monks and nuns—to engage in singing and dancing, however, according to Dzogchen, even a monk or nun, if they attain rigpa, can engage in singing and dancing and be in a place full of commotion and yet maintain rigpa and not break their vows. Breaking vows is relevant for a person who does not have rigpa; then an external code of ethics is necessary. If a person is completely aware internally, an external code of ethics is not required. Therefore, under those circumstances, a monastic can engage in unconventional behaviors and yet maintain their vows. That is what Saraha[17], one of the great mahasiddhas[18] has said.

Saraha came from the Brahman caste, the highest caste in India's social strata. He ran off with a girl from a disreputable outcast family. The community was shocked, especially the Buddhists. They could not understand why Saraha would do something that would cause so much embarrassment. Saraha said, "I wasn't a proper monk until I ran off with this woman." If we don't understand the philosophy of Saraha's actions and his ensuing comment, we may want to dismiss such activity as an abuse of Buddhism rather than propagating Buddhism. However, if we understood the philosophy behind such activities and choices, then we can understand why a person like Saraha acted in such a way, as the real precept is protecting one's mind from neurosis. A person who can protect their mind from neurosis does not need an external code of ethics to keep themselves in line, nor do they need the code of ethics that has been set down in the Buddhist tradition.

Chapter Six

Ethics and Meditation

The Origin of Buddhist Ethics

Buddha was a practical person. He was an empiricist of some kind, because the vinaya is composed of Buddha explaining to the monks what they could and could not do. Buddha did not sit down to write these ethical codes. Whenever a situation arose that created controversy or public outrage, the Buddha would instruct his monastics not to do that. A monastic may steal something, and Buddha would then add to the vinaya that "Stealing is not good." The Buddha developed these rules so his followers would cease discourteous action that created resentment and hostility in people's minds. As spiritual practitioners, such action should be restrained. A lot of the vinaya ethical codes are based upon discourteous behaviors, *drug de* in Tibetan, which means "group of six." All the vinaya rules are composed of actual incidents that took place in the Buddha's own time. They are a code of morals in that sense, but they don't have any superhuman origin, Buddha did not get it from someone else. The origin of Buddhist ethics comes from humans themselves. If human beings were less neurotic than they are, then there wouldn't be these types of moral precepts.

The basic ethic of even the vinaya is that of abiding by social convention, to refrain from doing things that would be regarded as unwholesome or discourteous by that particular society. For instance, in modern western society, if a monastic is following an ancient vinaya rule, but in the current context it is considered unwholesome or discourteous, that rule should be reviewed. That would not conflict with the way things are set out in the vinaya rules. There is nothing absolute in the rules themselves.

Buddha himself, in one of the sutras, said that the vinaya rules should be adapted to the time and place within a particular era. Therefore, one cannot be dogmatic about these rules as if they are absolute. There should not be rigid adherence to them under all circumstances. To be rigid would actually be to break the vinaya rule rather than preserve it. Then it would not benefit anybody. Because of one's self-righteous attitude, it would alienate the practitioner as well as alienating other people who may be interested in Buddhism. Rigid moral rules lead to a rigid way of thinking.

Looked at in that way, we can see the thrust and orientation of Buddhist practice in general, and Dzogchen practice in particular, is that of self-realization, self-actualization, and overcoming emotional disturbances of all kinds. That is the real orientation. A person could be a moralist and yet be the worst Buddhist that you could imagine, because the person has no peace of mind. One can become totally agitated and intolerant of those who don't share their views, and completely disturbed and neurotic about their moral standards. An obsessive adherence to a code of ethics has no place in Buddhism. Buddhist ethical codes do not have any type of theistic origins. In Buddhism, we see external codes of ethics as guides to interact meaningfully in the world. One should not be bound or conditioned by such a code because self-actualization becomes extremely difficult, and if one cannot become self-actualized and realized, then the whole orientation of Buddhism becomes abused. The goal of realization and enlightenment can completely slip from our hands.

Understanding oneself as one is, the concept of self-identity, or the concept of "I am," is extremely important in the Dzogchen tradition, and is known as the "Actuality of Being." The distinction between being and becoming is not made in the Dzogchen tradition—the being is the ground by which becoming is made possible.

In Dzogchen, as I have discussed, we do not need to renounce, purify, or transform anything. One is simply trying to understand how things are, how they exist just as they are, rather than seeing everything as primordially defective, both within oneself and externally. In the Dzogchen approach, we do not follow a process of rectification in order to gain spiritual awakenings.

The Dzogchen concept of human nature is grounded in the idea that a person is already perfect, but fails to realize the inherent perfection within oneself. The Dzogchen practices that are being presented here are based upon that particular principle. The practices are not designed to make one become better, healthier, more intelligent, or to disperse our confusions. Rather, despite our seeming imperfections and confusions, the practices are designed to help us realize that each person is a completely holistic person, a completely awakened person. Thus, in the Dzogchen tradition, the distinction between a samsaric human being and a fully evolved awakened person is not applicable. That is why it is called the "path of self-liberation."

If we understand our emotions properly, the emotions themselves are self-liberated without our needing to employ techniques to transform or get rid of them. Also, in Dzogchen we do not need to see the emotions as insubstantial or empty. Instead, if we understand how emotions manifest and operate, and gain deeper understanding of ourselves, we begin to realize that we do not need to become anything better. We can just simply be what we already are. In other words, we can try as hard as we like to become something other than what we already are, but that is not possible.

Approaching Meditation

We need to understand four concepts in order to practice Dzogchen meditation. The first three are *gnas, gyu, rigs,* and the fourth is *ying* in Tibetan. The first, gnas means stationary; when the mind is in a state of calmness, and not agitated. The second, gyu refers to the mind being in a state of movement, turmoil, or in other ways agitated. The third, *rigs* is bare awareness. Usually, in the Dzogchen vocabulary or terminology, it is called *nas gyu rig sum.*

It is very important to understand these concepts properly because usually in Buddhist meditation, and many other forms of meditation, it is said that we should aspire to attain calmness of mind. Further, we should try as much as possible, to be peaceful, and to have control of our emotions and other expressive outlets.

In Dzogchen meditation, it does not matter whether our mind is in a state of restfulness or agitation. Rigpa, or bare awareness, can never be realized if we make distinctions between our calm state of mind and our agitated state of mind. Therefore, if we experience emotional upheavals they should be simply seen as just that—nothing more, nothing less.

If we feel that whatever is taking place in the mind is dramatic, we do not have to determine whether it is real or not. Or if we regard our mental drama as just our interpreting our experience as dramatic, we do not have to determine whether it is real or not. It need not matter whether it is truly dramatic or not. We do not have to write a novel or thesis based on whether the thought processes or emotional upheavals that we experiencing are dramatic or not. We need not determine if they are real or not, based upon fantasies or have a source that we can trace back to—childhood, parental upbringing, education, and so on. All of that is of absolutely no consequence in Dzogchen meditation. What is important is simply to be able to remain with whatever state of mind appears, whether it is a calm or agitated state of mind. These are the first three concepts, nas gyu rig sum, to be understood for Dzogchen meditation.

The fourth is the concept of "ying," which is often translated as "sphere," but it means something more like "field," or "horizon." Ying has a somewhat spatial connotation. It does not mean outside space, as we normally understand it. It is rather, some kind of psychological space but it is not confined within a body. The spaciousness is non-differential to inner and outer or subject and object—both reside in the notion of ying. The concept of ying is introduced so we do not see the mind as small, encased within the body and completely cramped up full of all kinds of mental activities. Rather, we experience the mind as completely limitless and spacious. The concept of ying relates to the mind-in-itself, the ground of being, the "I am." As far as self-identity or "I am" is concerned, it is seen as undetermined. It is an all-encompassing field, an all-encompassing horizon.

Even when one finds their mind cluttered up with thoughts, emotions, and sensations of all kinds, one manages to not entangle oneself in that state. The practitioner realizes that what is taking place is the mind in the state of ying. We need to realize that we can never reduce our mind or consciousness simply to imagination, memory, thoughts, emotions, and so forth. There is a wider field or horizon always present. In Dzogchen meditation, we are trying to remain in a that mode of being, so we are not disturbed by either calmness or agitation, understanding that calmness does not necessarily lead to boredom, or agitation lead to despair.

When the whole thing is looked at from that point of view, meditation in this particular context has nothing to do with cultivating what one would normally regard as a meditative state of mind. It also has nothing to do with discarding a lot of causes and conditions which one regards as leading to a disruptive state of mind. As stated in the Dzogchen texts, we should neither discard, *pang* in Tibetan, or cultivate, *lang* in Tibetan. Therefore, in meditation, we should try not to cultivate any state of mind, nor should we try to discard any state of mind we might find ourselves in.

What that fundamentally means is we should have a totally open attitude towards ourselves, which we normally do not have. The starting point to be able to interact with other human beings and our external environment properly is to find that total openness with ourselves. Unless we are totally open with ourselves, no matter how much we try to be open to others, it becomes a contrived and diluted form of openness—not deliberately, but inadvertently. Deliberately one might want to be extremely gentle, understanding, and so forth, but all of those wishes can be diluted if we are not willing to face up to ourselves. We may feel there are dangerous or demonic forces that we need to protect ourselves from and therefore we cannot afford to look within ourselves with such openness. From the Dzogchen perspective, that is not the case.

To gain any understanding of ourselves, we need to open to ourselves and reveal a total picture of what we are. Only then can we gain any insight into mind-in-itself, the ground of being. This is why the Dzogchen approach is called the "path of self-liberation," rather than the "path of transformation." It is called the path of self-liberation because one is not trying to transform negative states of mind into positive states of mind, trying to cultivate virtuous states of mind, or trying to cultivate other kinds of spiritual qualities, in the conventional sense. That does not make us less spiritual; it gives us a total perspective on ourselves. If we shun certain aspects of ourselves and cultivate others, we create a blindness or darkness of who we are and what we are like. Other people might be able to see what we are doing, thinking, and how we are behaving. Our seemly best inner-kept secrets often manifest through our actions and interactions with other people. Others can often see the parts of ourselves we do not want to have anything to do with, the parts we are blind to and disengaged from.

In Dzogchen meditation, we should be becoming more familiar with our positivities and negativities. The positive sides are not necessarily cultivated with a great deal of effort as that is not needed in Dzogchen meditation. What is required is to just simply sit and be aware. Effort is unnecessary because effort can be a distraction to awareness. We can easily deviate from this original purpose. We can become so embroiled in how we think we should be meditating, or what thoughts we think we should be having, that the meditation practice becomes full of distraction and can disrupt our meditation practice altogether.

This is the starting point for Dzogchen meditation, recognizing we can experience more freedom if we allow things to happen in the mind, rather than always thinking, "I should be doing more, or I should be doing something different." If we continually feel that we should be making effort one way or another, our meditation experience becomes less and less free. Further, we can feel as if our whole life is controlled by our own and others expectations, and a range of other external circumstances. Continual effort to be something other can create feelings of being boxed in, trapped, or oppressed. Instead, one begins to have this experience of complete lack of freedom.

We begin to realize that all the limitations that we often attribute to the outside world—external situations and circumstances—are nothing other than a mode of interpretation conjured up by the mind. Our limitation can be seen as nothing other than our mental interpretations. How trapped and restricted we feel depends on how we manage our own mind. For example, we can be in the same situation at different times of our lives; at one time we may feel bogged down or trapped and at another time not feel trapped at all.

In Dzogchen meditation, through awareness, we allow our

minds this sense of freedom. When one feels free, responsibility goes hand in hand with this experience. We take responsibility for whatever emotional experience we may be facing in our meditation. We cannot be free unless we take responsibility for ourselves as well. We want freedom, yet at the same time, when freedom is presented, we may recoil because we do not want to take full responsibility for ourselves. We cannot have one without the other. We need to take responsibility for our feelings of limitation, as well as feelings of entrapment. Feelings of inadequacy and entrapment derive from misunderstanding ourselves. This occurs when we deviate from our actual state of being.

Chapter Seven

The Four Yogas, Meditation, and Mental Clarity

The Four Yogas

From the Dzogchen perspective, we see ourselves as fundamentally pure even though we may not recognize it. The practice develops an understanding, or at least a glimpse of the possibility of our being fundamentally pure. The four yogas assist us with this understanding. Yoga in this particular context is not referring to working with the body, but rather working with one's true condition, to gain contact with one's true nature.[19]

The first yoga is called "yoga of one pointedness," *tse chik* in Tibetan, *ekagra* in Sanskrit. Most people who have done meditation at one time or another would most likely find the term "one pointed state of mind" quite familiar. We may often think of one pointed concentration as a singular focus entailing a state of mind devoid of thoughts, emotions, and concepts. Another view of one pointed concentration is to contemplate emptiness, or the insubstantiality of things. Removing all immediate concerns of the relative world through either blocking mental activity or only concentrating on insubstantiality is not in concert with the Dzogchen view of one pointed concentration.

According to Dzogchen, one pointed concentration does not require us to empty our minds of thoughts, ideas, and emotions, but rather to rest one's mind while the mind is in movement or agitated. Normally, it can be easier to empty our mind of activities to create a "state of tranquility." However, in Dzogchen, it is not a matter of discarding our thoughts, as much as being able to rest with our thoughts. It is known as the "indivisibility of transformation, change, and rest," in regard to mental activities. There is no division seen between the mind that is completely rested and calm, and the mind that is active. When we begin to see the mind in that way, when thoughts arise, they do not agitate the mind. That is what is referred to by the yoga of one pointedness, and the Dzogchen practitioner relates to their mind in that way.

The second is the "yoga of non-discrimination," *tros dral* in Tibetan, *aprapanca* in Sanskrit. It is linked to one pointed concentration in that one does not discriminate between one's mental states seeing some states as conducive to the attainment of nirvana, and others as not conducive. In meditation, we do not discriminate in terms of what we experience. When we cease to make such sharp distinctions and suspend our judgments, the experiences can manifest by themselves. We can then realize that what we normally regard as immediate experience is not immediate at all. We realize that what is so called immediate is actually a product of our conceptual processes. We should practice non-discriminative yoga, because when we do not discriminate, we allow experiences to arise rather than creating our experiences habitually.

The third is the "yoga of one flavor," or "yoga of one taste," *ro chik* in Tibetan, *ekerasa* in Sanskrit. By transitioning through the two previous yogas, we come to realize that all our experiences are permeated by emptiness or insubstantiality, whether positive, negative, good, bad, wholesome, or unwholesome. Everything we experience has the same flavor, the flavor of emptiness. We begin to develop the attitude of non-acceptance (not accepting certain experiences as being totally wonderful), and non-rejection (not rejecting some experiences as being totally bad). Non-acceptance and non-rejection are extraordinarily important practices in

Dzogchen. Not because accepting and rejecting things are bad per se. Usually, what we accept and reject are conditioned by what we have learned and experienced in the past. Our acceptances and rejections are contingent on karmic traces and dispositions developed over time by all kinds of misguided and preconceived ideas.

The fourth is the "yoga of non-meditation," *gom med* in Tibetan, *abhavana* in Sanskrit. The ultimate aim of Dzogchen practice is to not distinguish between meditation and non-meditation, as meditation itself can be a contrived activity. When one is fully present with full awareness, whether one is meditating or not, there is no difference. Being fully present all the time, whether asleep or awake, walking or sitting, they are always present. That is called the yoga of non-meditation. It could also be called meditation in everyday life. Whatever task one is involved in, they are not distracted, but rather fully present and in a meditative state.

The Significance of the Pause in Body, Speech, and Mind

As has already been stated, the first eight yanas of the nine yana system deal with the ordinary, everyday consciousness, whereas the ninth yana deals with one's existential being, or mind-in-itself. It should also be emphasized that Dzogchen practice is not designed to discover how the mind works, and the basic structure of the consciousness. The emphasis is on the realization of body, speech, and mind. We work with our body by engaging in yogic exercises of all kinds, including the vajra posture that I will elaborate on later in the book.

"The dissolution of the meditative state" is used in Dzogchen terminology to describe a practitioner who has overcome conceptualization, and gone beyond such distinctions as a calm state and a turbulent state of mind, a meditative and non-meditative state, and so on. They are able to go beyond that. They are no longer bound by situations or concepts that relate to boundaries, and their meditative state becomes unceasing, regardless of what they are engaged in.

Each concept that relates to boundaries is a limitation in itself. For instance, if a transcendentally orientated person wishes to transcend their immediate situation of bondage or samsara, a conceptual boundary has been created. Further, if we decide life is pretty good as is, apart from sporadic upheavals, and we do not need to look into our lives or understand ourselves, another conceptual boundary has been created.

In the Dzogchen tradition, all boundary concepts are broken down, including the distinction of seeing oneself as an afflicted, ordinary sentient creature, and that one must become an enlightened, awakened person. All such boundary concepts need to be transcended, and eventually the ideas of meditation and non-meditation are also transcended, or dissolved.

When it comes to the activities of body and speech, we need to pay more attention to pauses. We usually do not think that pauses are important, whether we are thinking, saying, or doing something. While we tend to ignore pauses completely, it is difficult to imagine speaking or acting without pauses. Pauses are extremely important. Once we begin to pay attention to the pauses or gaps, ying, the notion of the spaciousness that pervades all of our activities, begins to make much more sense.

When we begin to pay attention to the pauses, we become much more aware of what we are doing with our bodies and our speech. For instance, in practicing different yogic exercises, the exercises can be punctuated with a particular gap or pause. As it is with speech, such as the recitation of mantras, each mantric utterance is punctuated with pauses. After practicing in this way, our everyday experience can be affected. There is no real point in simply doing yogic exercises or reciting mantras without it being translated into our everyday experience. The punctuation or pauses are the most important in terms of what we are experiencing.

It is a matter of understanding that our body, speech, and mind are integrated in relation to ying. The pauses represent ying—the horizon, the encompassment. There is nothing that is not pervaded by ying. If we do not pay attention to the pauses, the gaps, the intermediate stages, we lose sight of the whole. If we pay more attention to the gaps or pauses within our actions, our actions can become less compulsive. The reason our actions are compulsive is because we do not allow ourselves to have any gaps, any pauses, in our actions. The reason why our speech is compulsive is because we do not allow any gaps in order to see what is being said or spoken of.

Carrying one's meditation into everyday life has to do with maintaining awareness of the pauses. Without this, we cannot build awareness of our daily activities. Without this spill effect over into our daily life, what we do with our body, speech, and mind cannot really be classed as meditative practice.

By engaging in the practice of Dzogchen, one begins to become dispossessed of all the karmic traces, dispositions, and intellectual perplexity, which is called *vikalpa* in Sanskrit, *nam tog* in Tibetan. It is due to vikalpa that it is difficult for the mind-in-itself to be revealed, or unconcealed. When the many layers of concepts—and concepts of concepts, and concepts of concepts of concepts—are removed, our mind becomes more and more aware as a natural consequence, and rigpa is able to manifest. That does not mean we are not in touch with rigpa, mind-in-itself, or basic being. It simply means, when all the adventitious obstacles, *lo bur gyi drib pa* in Tibetan, are removed, it is much easier to understand what our true being is.

When we are not yet dispossessed of our karmic traces and dispositions, but are aware of the gap or pause—between the previous thought that has just gone, and the coming thought yet manifested—within our meditation, we can recognize that gap as none other than our basic being. Mind-in-itself, rigpa, or bare awareness, is already present in such a gap. Whether the gap is long or short is relative. It is a gap that the Dzogchen practitioner is trying to maintain. At the same time, I should emphasize that we are not trying to rid ourselves of thoughts.

What one is trying to realize is called *jung nas dro sum* in Tibetan. There are three modes in which thought operates. The first is the origin of thought, the second is the presentness of thought, and the third is when the thought has disappeared. When we begin to become aware of those three modes, jung nas dro sum, we begin to realize that a thought originates from mind-in-itself, the nature of mind, or our basic being. The thought is present and then it naturally dissolves by itself, which is called "self-liberation." It disperses back into mind-in-itself. Therefore, one does not need to create this duality of thoughts, on the one hand, and whatever state of mind we might be trying to cultivate, on the other hand. Those two situations are brought together.

In Dzogchen, there are various modes of the liberation of thoughts and different metaphors are given to illustrate these.

1. Meeting an old friend
   Initially, liberating a thought or emotion is like meeting an old friend. A thought or emotion appears, it triggers some kind of reaction, but then one recognizes the situation in the same way one would recognize an old friend and remembers to release it.

2. A snake unknotting itself
   When a thought occurs, by leaving it to itself, it will at some point be freed naturally, like a snake unknotting itself from its coils.

3. A drawing on water
   A thought will arise and cause slight disturbance but immediately vanishes within itself, in the same way a drawing

on the surface of water immediately vanishes the very instant it
is written.

4. A thief entering an empty house
   Finally, one becomes free from hope and fear about whether or
   not thoughts arise, in the same way a thief entering an empty
   house finds there is nothing to steal and immediately leaves.

Two Types of Mental States

All the experiences that we have during meditation can be
reduced to two types of mental states—rest and movement. The
variety of experiences we have can be subsumed under the two
categories. Through meditation practice, we develop awareness and
begin to harmonize these different types of experiences—
movement of thoughts or concepts and the restful, calm,
tranquility state are normally experienced as two conflicting types
of experience. With the development of awareness, we can begin
to have a more unified, total, all-encompassing, non-partial
experience. The development of non-partiality means we do not
exclude some experiences and cultivate others.

As mentioned, in Dzogchen meditation, we don't judge or filter
our experiences, but rather let our experiences manifest without
interference or conditioning. This in turn allows our sensory
experiences to be free of interference as well. We do not have to
block out or exaggerate sensory presentations of sight, sound, touch,
smell, or taste, but simply let the sensory experiences be. This can
only happen when our mind is left at rest. Often we can feel external
objects and sensory presentations such as physical and visual objects
and sound are impinging on us. By engaging in meditation, we
discover how we normally perceive the external world is
predominantly constructed by our mind due to our concepts, ideas,
and conceptual categorization of all kinds. When we let our mind
be, the sensory presentations are left to themselves, they just are.

That is why the distinction is made in Dzogchen of the appearance and things as they actually are. Normally what we perceive and experience is just a construction of our own mind. It is simply the way things appear to us personally. If we let our mind be without conceptual categorization of our perceptions going on, we allow ourselves to experience the way things are. That is why the emphasis on letting our mind simply "be" is encouraged. As a result of letting the sensory presentations be without blocking them out or indulging in them, but simply being present with what one is experiencing, then it becomes enjoyment. Not enjoyment in an indulgent sense, but rather a sublime enjoyment. Experiencing the world through our senses assumes a whole new dimension beyond our normal sensory presentations or sense pleasures. It turns into a total spiritual experience.

Depression and Elation in Relation to Mental Clarity

We might feel we encounter many difficulties and obstacles during meditation. The list of obstacles to mental clarity or meditation can be infinite. However, all our experiences that lead us away from mental clarity or meditation come under two categories: depression,[20] *jing wa* in Tibetan, *laya* in Sanskrit; and elation, *godh pa* in Tibetan and *uddhatya* in Sanskrit.

With depression or despondency, we can lose the capacity to take interest and explore. It is important to distinguish depression from despair. We often associate depression with feelings of despairing. If we don't see much point in anything, we can give up and as a result we suffer from depression. However, despair can provide a jolt and wake us up, whereas depression has the opposite effect, it makes us go to sleep, sometimes literally and other times metaphorically.

According to the Dzogchen viewpoint, there are four principle reasons why a person has a depressive or despondent state of mind.

1. A person could feel depressed because of a time. Sometimes it just happens that we are in a depressive mood, and there is no particular reason why one is in a depressive state of mind.

2. A person could feel depressed because of a particular action. One may behave in a particularly negative way, perpetrating their actions bringing harm to someone else. This can lead to a depressive state.

3. A person could become depressed, not due to perpetuating a time of sadness or a negative action, though these could pre-empt mental instability, *drib* in Tibetan. All mental imbalances, neurosis, psychosis, et cetera are called drib. Mental instability is seen as a much more complex and persistent cause of depression.

4. A person could be depressed because it is built into that person's personality, *nam min* in Tibetan, which refers to their general karmic disposition. Some people are more depressively disposed than others, which can be worked with in meditation.

With the last two types of depression listed, one needs to develop an understanding of how the karmic mechanisms are operating, and how the neuroses are affecting the way in which one behaves. The first two—time and action, would be indirectly worked with if we were working with the last two.

There is a particular meditative visualization technique that is used in Dzogchen to be able to deal with depression.[19]

Meditation

Settle yourself on a comfortable cushion or chair, resting the mind gently for a short time, then begin the visualization:

Visualize a small red ball of light above your head. The light descends and enters your body and fills up the whole body with red glowing light. The color red is used as it gives a sense of lightening up, a sense of rising upwards, and a sense of opening up. A depressive state of mind tends to close up and a person can feel detachment, closing off, and disengaging. The red light is supposed to help open up our state of mind to become more expansive, rising up instead of being depressed, which literally means being pressed down. As the light fills up your whole body with light, the light begins to radiate outwards. All the depression becomes part of the light itself. It radiates outwards and begins to glow within and around you, in the atmosphere. One remains in that particular state. When the visualization comes to an end one can remain with a sense of feeling uplifted and spacious.

The other aspect is elation, the opposite of feeling depressed. Elation here does not mean being happy or joyful, it is more to do with an agitated state of mind. When the mind is running all over the place, cluttered up with all kinds of thoughts and emotions, then the mind is not at rest at all. Such agitation makes it difficult to have clarity of mind, because we have no means of bringing about mental calmness.

Meditation

Settle yourself on a comfortable cushion or chair, resting the mind gently for a short time, then begin the visualization:

Visualize a blue light on top of one's head. As in the previous method, the blue light descends and enters one's body, fills up one's entire body, and radiates out. The English word "elation" is very appropriate here; it has the connotation of going upward. The color blue is visualized and the energy comes down, so the mind has to calm down rather than rise upwards. The color blue automatically has that feeling, a soothing quality and a coolness attached to that.

Depression and elation have some relation to Dzogchenpas' approach to shamatha or tranquility meditation, and vipashyana or insight meditation. They say that shamatha can deal with agitation and elation, and vipashyana deals with the depressive mind. Shamatha is seen as having an effect of coolness, or calming down the agitated mind. In vipashyana, one develops awareness that rises up and can therefore cut through depression.

These techniques used to deal with these two states of mind should be used sparingly in Dzogchen practice. If one experiences either one of these obstacles, the technique can be used to overcome that mental state to then resume the meditation of allowing whatever arises in the mind to be. In Dzogchen, these techniques are used as a last resort and should only be used if we are unable to stay with our depression and elation and avoid judgment—acceptance or rejection of our experiences—as much as possible. This is particularly important in Dzogchen—not to accept thoughts of the Buddha, meditation, renunciation, or reject thoughts of anger, jealousy, and so on. One should let things be and not condition them in any way, not feel this is depressive mind or this is agitated mind, and not try to work something out about all the things one is experiencing. Just allow them to arise and just be with them. If one does this effectively, then one would gain *togpa*, which means understanding the workings of the mind.

Chapter Eight

Integration of Bliss, Luminosity, and Reality

Yugananda is a Sanskrit word which means "union," "unity," or "coming-togetherness." The notion of unity, or non-conceptuality, in relation to bliss, clarity or luminosity, and reality, are intimately related to the general Buddhist understanding of the three *kayas*. The aspect of non-conceptuality in relation to bliss is connected with the nirmanakaya, or manifest aspect of Buddha's being. The non-conceptuality aspect of clarity, or luminosity, is related with the sambogakaya, or the communicative aspect of Buddha's being. The non-conceptuality of reality is connected with the dharmakaya, or the authentic state of Buddha's being. One has to understand those three types of non-conceptuality in relation to these three aspects of Buddha's embodied being. All of those experiences of non-conceptuality are described as *nyam*, which will be discussed later.

Non-conceptuality of bliss and emptiness

The first type of non-conceptuality is known as "non-conceptuality of bliss and emptiness," *de tong* in Tibetan, and that is concerned with the non-conceptual experience of pleasure. In Dzogchen, pleasure is cultivated rather than discarded or ignored, so there is a particular practice that a person does in order to bring this about. This is particularly connected with the notion of body. Normally, we think we are experiencing physical pleasure, but we may not be. Generally, we distinguish between being healthy and sickness, seeing healthy as the absence of sickness. According to Dzogchen thought, health is not just the absence of sickness, as both are seen as just concepts. In the same way, our concept of sanity and insanity would also be relative. Genuine health goes beyond our ordinary notions of health and sickness.

According to the Dzogchen way of thinking, a person who completely understands themselves, and is completely in touch with themselves, is fully sane. Someone who is simply coping and able to function in the world would not be seen as being someone who is particularly sane. Like pleasure and pain, it is a relative concept.

With this particular practice, one is trying to cultivate a sense of transcendental pleasure, or transcendental bliss, in order to bring the mind and body together. We need both body and mind to experience pleasure or bliss. Pleasure or bliss provides the only opportunity to bring the mind and body together harmoniously, as there is no conflict going on within ourselves, and no disharmonious conditions are being created.

Working with one's body in this way helps our body become less rigid and pre-programmed. Relating to our body in a conventional way results in our body becomeing mechanical. Repetitive movements can be damaging or unhealthy, taking attentiveness of our bodies away. For example, if there is a lot of repetition at work, such as spending many hours sitting in an office chair, one may suffer back pain or other ailments. We all share this type of experience. Such experiences come from not being able to experience the body properly, experience pleasure properly, and being unable to properly connect the mind and the body. It may be difficult to say we actually experience pleasure physically. We may say that when having sex, at least we are saved for a short time; we have connected with our experience. Even that becomes suspicious. Even that can become mechanized. If we review the way in which people look at sex, it can be seen as very mechanical.

We may believe we live in a more liberated society and sex is no longer taboo, but have we created another distortion of the sexual experience? Much has been written and discussed about how to learn about and approach sex, and that type of attitude is quite prevalent. According to Dzogchen, such an attitude towards our body and its performance is misguided and misjudged, and it deprives us of pleasure. For example, if the whole emphasis is put on performance, as if it is such a great feat that is to be performed, then one may be constantly focused on performing really well and forget about sex in the genuine sense of the word. In Dzogchen practice, sex is discussed and seen as having the potential to enhance an understanding of the body and mind, the link between the two, and the cultivation of bliss.

The approach is to be present and allow oneself to feel and experience, rather than loading all kinds of constraints and demands on ourselves as we normally do. That is seen as the reason we experience less and less pleasure and tend to go from one interest or intrigue to the next in search of pleasure, trying to find that which can give us lasting pleasure. We mechanize our experiences and become bored, motivating us to switch to something else, something new. The same repetitive procedure ensues, as we lose touch with our experiences in general.

In Dzogchen practice and other forms of tantric practice, the cultivation of pleasure is seen as a component of the practice. When one experiences proper pleasure, one is in a contented state of mind. If one is not experiencing pleasure, one is generally not in a contented state of mind. This leads to all kinds of disturbances of the mind. Even the practice itself, if mechanized, can become an obstacle, rather than enhancing one's development. An example of a tantric practice designed to generate pleasure is the practice of *tummo*, or mystic heat yoga. Tummo literally means "the fierce one." Tummo is more feminine, so it really means "fierce woman." The mystic heat practice is done purely for this purpose.[21]

Meditation

Settle yourself on a comfortable cushion or chair, resting the mind gently for a short time, then begin the visualization:

A simplified form of tummo practice is to visualize white liquid in the crown center. The white liquid is almost dripping. Then one visualizes a central channel, the thickness of a drinking straw, which is blue—a straight channel going into the cortex and coming down and finishing three or four inches below the navel. One then visualizes fire at the navel center. The white liquid that one visualizes in the crown center is seen as the male element, and the fire in the navel center is seen as the female element. What one is trying to do is to integrate the two and in the process generate bliss or pleasure. One has to heat up the fire and really feel that this very strong heat activity is going on there. That heat from the fire element gradually rises up and goes into the crown chakra and starts to melt the liquid. The liquid passes through the throat and heart chakras and finally lands in the navel chakra—so the liquid is absorbed into the fire. As the liquid passes through those different energy centers or chakras, one should generate as much pleasure as one can summon and really try to feel that, let the pleasure pervade all of one's body, not conceptualize or think about anything else other than what one is visualizing. One pays more attention to the visual side and the feeling tone side of the whole process, rather than on the conceptual or thinking part. Let the sensation absorb oneself and physically try to feel and generate it. By doing this, one is integrating one's body and mind, as well as the male and female elements within oneself. It is a way of cutting through our dualistic notions of all sorts.

Dzogchen practice in itself is about integration, engagement, and union. It is a holistic approach. One can do this in tummo through the generation of mystic heat. The approach to take with this practice is the non-conceptual aspect of the pleasure.

Non-conceptuality of Clarity and Emptiness

The second aspect of non-conceptuality is called the "non-conceptuality of clarity and emptiness," *sal tong* in Tibetan. What this refers to is the clarity or the luminous aspect of the mind, which comes after developing pleasure or bliss. When the body is completely integrated, the mind becomes clear. When our body is rigid, our mind is also rigid and narrowed. When our mind is narrow, it is agitated. If the body is well composed, then the mind also becomes clear. It becomes non-conceptually clear and it shows through our body as well. This is a point that can often be misunderstood. That is, when Dzogchenpas talk about clarity, it is not just a purely mental phenomenon, it is also a body phenomenon. A person might begin to radiate or show all kinds of signs of non-conceptual clarity. This is particularly perceptible when we look at high beings such as His Holiness the Dalai Lama. A person begins to radiate and glow. These are not just metaphors, this is an actual experience that can be perceived by others.

Non-conceptuality of clarity does not mean that we should not conceptualize, or avoid thoughts coming into our mind, or avoid experiencing emotions within the state of meditation. It means completely the opposite. It means letting thoughts and emotions arise and just being able to be with these mental processes as they happen, and avoid judgments or interpretations of these arisings, but simply let ourselves experience whatever the emotions or thought processes that one is experiencing.

From the Dzogchen perspective, we can't work with emotions. This is a very interesting approach because we are always working on something, especially when we deal with emotions. In Dzogchen practice, there is nothing to work on. Emotions themselves are not seen as the problem. The way we go about relating to the emotions is seen as the problem. According to Dzogchen, we should let the emotions be, undisturbed by our judgments and desire to transform them into something better. When we begin to approach emotions in that way, we can begin to realize that emotions themselves are part of the transcendental aspect of one's own consciousness. That is, there is no limit to transcendental consciousness, therefore emotions are permeated by the transcendental region of the consciousness so they should not be rejected or cultivated. They should be left alone.

Meditation

Settle yourself on a comfortable cushion or chair, resting the mind gently for a short time, then begin the exercise:

In this meditation exercise, we deliberately think of something that would instigate a negative emotional feeling, such as anger, desire, jealousy, or pride, et cetera. We let the emotions arise and then deliberately build that emotional feeling. Then we contrast the negative feelings by generating a positive emotion such as love. For example, we can deliberately create an angry state of mind. Having done that, we can then think of someone that we care for very much. Then we try to remain with the particular state of mind we have created. In effect, we create varieties of emotional states of mind and remain with them for a time.

What is interesting about this practice is that we normally go from one emotional state to another, but are not aware of the transitional stage. We do not usually see how different states of mind arise because our attention is not persistent enough. However, in a practice such as this, we are deliberately creating different types of emotions and states of mind, and can observe the texture and feeling tone of the emotional reactions with immediacy.

We can begin to realize that the contrasting emotional experiences are not so different after all. We can find a lot of similarities between the feeling of anger, love, jealousy, and compassion. The emotional experiences that we normally regard as being poles apart are not so, and one comes to the realization of some kind of basic, fundamental texture of all emotions. Therefore, one no longer regards some emotions as being positive that have to be obsessively cultivated, and other emotions as bad and have to be gotten rid of. One can allow varieties of emotional experiences to manifest and then let them be without cultivating or rejecting them. We should keep in mind that according to the Dzogchen tradition, emotions are not regarded as separate from concepts.

Normally, we think when we are emotional, we have lost control and we use our concepts— then everything is under control and worked out, so we are afraid that we will lose our reasoning power if we become too emotional. This is the interesting split that we make, that emotions have more to do with our biological responses and are much more physical, whereas concepts are related to our mental activity, so they are superior to the basic emotional feelings. In Dzogchen, that distinction is not made.

Emotions and concepts go together, one cannot have emotions without concepts and vice versa. Every time we have an emotional experience, there is a concept associated with that. Even though there might be transcultural experience of emotions, nonetheless, a person experiences emotions in accordance with conditioning within their society. For example, a Tibetan person's anger might be different from a western person's anger because of the conceptual framework employed to relate to the emotions. When the Dzogchen method is being employed, instead of looking at one's emotions from a particular conceptual framework, one tries to gain immediate experience of the emotions as they present. We try to experience anger, or love, et cetera just as it is, instead of seeing love from a particular viewpoint and experiencing anger from another viewpoint. In Dzogchen practice, we let the emotion arise unaided and without interference. When one practices in this way, one realizes that emotions are also constructions of our mind, they don't just happen to us.

The western usage of the word "emotion," and "passion," et cetera connote a type of passivity. The word "emotion" comes from the Latin word "emovere," which means a state of being moved, agitated, or perturbed. This kind of description of emotion suggests we may be passive victims of our emotions and thus not fully responsible for them. At the same time, it removes the experience of the emotion out of the picture completely. Our emotional experiences are often described as, "I was overwhelmed with anger," or "I was torn apart," as if emotions are doing the tearing, or, "I was overcome with emotion," or "I was bogged down by my feelings," as if we have no responsibility towards our emotions. Fear of emotions can be generated from such an approach and attitude. If we articulate how we experience emotions in that way, it can tend to make us feel less of a sense of responsibility. We can feel we have less freedom, giving more weight to the emotions than they deserve. In that way, our emotional experience can become overwhelming. However, if we can let the emotions arise as they do, and not think the emotions are going to overwhelm us, or that they are going to make us lose our reasoning power, that they are going to tear us apart or bog us down, then we begin to develop a completely different understanding.

When one begins to let emotions arise, and not use any particular antidotes to get rid of them, but deliberately create emotional situations in meditation, we can see, "I can make myself feel angry, I can make myself feel loving, proud, depressed." In this way, we begin to see how and why we we go about doing the kinds of things that we do, and we can also have first-hand experience of emotions, which we do not have most of the time. Normally, by the time we get to see our emotions, it is already a second-hand experience. It has already passed through our filtering process. We experience anger, jealousy, pride or any other emotions with some kind of pre-determined pre-emptive response. This type of tension accompanies our emotional experience and is testimony to our indirect and distorted emotional experience. They are not experienced properly or fully. If we did experience emotions properly, there would be no tension. There would be no disturbances of any sort.

Once we begin to let ourselves experience emotions and just let them be without contrivance or distortion, we can have a much clearer mind because concepts and emotions are intimately related. Since concepts and emotions are intimately related, if we allow those activities to happen in the mind without obstruction, the natural consequence of that type of manifestation is the experience of luminosity or clarity.

Non-conceptuality of Reality

The third aspect is known as "non-conceptuality of reality," which is non-conceptuality of ying, or field. Once these processes have been accomplished and the person begins to enter into the state of the non-conceptuality of the field, or ying, that is considered the final stage of Dzogchen and that is what Dzogchen really means. Dzogchen is the name given to the ultimate experience of the person, the final integration of the person. The person has been able to integrate subject and object, overcome dualities of all kinds—good and bad, sickness and health, sanity and insanity, and so on. When the person has moved beyond that and is able to reside in the ying, then they are completely fulfilled. There is nothing else to be done, and therefore it is Dzogchen, which means completely fulfilled.

Three Methods of Integration

These three methods of integration and the methods presented previously may seem as though they are in direct conflict with the path of self-liberation. Since there is nothing to be transformed, cultivated, or rejected, how can we reconcile these methods of integration to the Dzogchen approach of self-liberation? The explanation is that Dzogchenpas can make use of the path of transformation whenever it is necessary. One does not need to become fanatical about Dzogchen practice. One does not have to be engrossed in the path of self-liberation so to refuse to have anything to do with the path of transformation. Whenever we have difficulties on the path, we can utilize certain practices of the anuyoga tantra, the highest tantric practice.

These methods of integration are designed to work with a particular emotion. In Buddhist practice, the two fundamental emotions that all the other emotions manifest from are desire and aggression, both of which arise from self-deception or ignorance. Each method of integration deals with one of those states of mind. Bliss deals with desire; luminosity deals with aggression; and the integration of rigpa deals with ignorance.

As discussed, in the Buddhist teachings, the emotions are not seen as some kind of external or internal force. The emotions are intimately related to our concepts, ideas, judgments, and even our reasoning capacity. Emotions should also be distinguished from feelings. One can have an emotional experience and that may have some effect on one's physiological processes yet, at the same time, emotions are not physiological and they are not feelings as well. In this context, feelings are completely involuntary. If we feel pain or hunger or thirst, whatever the case might be, they come and go at their own will, so to speak. With emotions, depending upon what sort of assessments and judgments we make about the situation, our emotions would also go through different states and varieties of experiences as a result of those considerations.

Integration of Bliss

This is the second tummo practice presented in this book. It has similarities to the early practice described, nonetheless, there are subtle differences and it should therefore be regarded as a separate but related practice.

Meditation

Settle yourself on a comfortable cushion or chair, resting the mind gently for a short time, then begin the visualization:

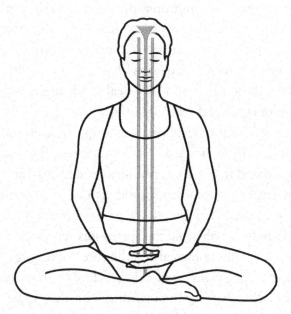

One visualizes three energy pathways, three straight tubes the thickness of a drinking straw, right, left, and center in the middle of the body. The right is white, the left is red, and the central one is light blue externally and red inside. They are translucent. The top part of the central channel goes right up to the skull and opens out like the top of a funnel. The other part terminates at the anus. Having visualized that, one starts to visualize a small flame at the level of the abdomen. As the flame begins to generate heat, one visualizes nectar dripping down, which is both red and white. When the nectar starts to drip it lands at the heart center and gradually the central channel expands so that it begins to incorporate both of the other channels. Then one has to visualize that the central channel has encompassed the totality of one's being and one is completely saturated in the nectar. One is still concentrating at the heart center and one starts to generate bliss as a result of that and remains within that blissful experience. One remains in meditation within that particular state for a while before moving on to the integration of luminosity meditation.

Integration of Luminosity
Meditation

Settle yourself on a comfortable cushion or chair, resting the mind gently for a short time, then begin the visualization:

In the integration of luminosity visualization, there is a slight difference in terms of visualizing the three channels as was done in the second tummo meditation.

First, one visualizes three energy pathways, three straight tubes the thickness of a drinking straw, right, left, and center in the middle of the body. The right is white, the left is red, and the central one is light blue externally and red inside. They are translucent. Different to the tummo practice, the two outer channels do not remain parallel but curve in and join the central channel following the skull line. Then they curve down and terminate at the end of the nostrils. Having visualized that, one then visualizes a ball of light at the heart center. One breathes out gently, then breathes in very, very slowly, and then breathes out with a certain amount of force. One resumes normal breathing, and while one visualizes, the light ball gradually begins to become more and more radiant. It starts to grow until it begins to illuminate the whole of one's body. The light starts to assume five different colors—red, yellow, blue, green, and white. Once the colored lights have illuminated the whole of one's body, they begin to contract into the point at the heart center. One remains in meditation within that particular state for a while before moving on to the integration of rigpa meditations.

Integration of Rigpa, or Non-conceptuality
Meditation 1

Settle yourself on a comfortable cushion or chair, resting the mind gently for a short time, then begin the visualization:

Again, one visualizes three energy pathways, three straight tubes the thickness of a drinking straw, right, left, and center in the middle of the body. The right is white, the left is red, and the central one is light blue externally and red inside. They are translucent. The two outer channels do not remain parallel but curve in and join the central channel following the skull line. Then they curve down and terminate at the end of the nostrils. Maintaining that visualization, one breathes out gently, then breathes in very, very slowly, and then breathes out with a certain amount of force. One then resumes normal breathing, and visualizes a ball of light at the heart center. From the heart center, the ball of light shoots up from the heart center, along the central channel and through the skull, ejecting through the crown center, shooting into the space and then dissolving into the space. One then remains in that state for a time.

Meditation 2

As in the previously, one visualizes three energy pathways, three straight tubes the thickness of a drinking straw, right, left, and center in the middle of the body. The right is white, the left is red, and the central one is light blue externally and red inside. They are translucent. The two outer channels do not remain parallel but curve in and join the central channel following the skull line. Then they curve down and terminate at the end of the nostrils. Maintaining that visualization, one breathes out gently, then breathes in very, very slowly, and then breathes out with a certain amount of force. One resumes normal breathing, and visualizes a ball of light at the heart center. From the heart center, the ball of light shoots up along the central channel and through the skull, ejecting through the crown center, and shooting into the space and then dissolving into the space.

In this second method, while remaining in the state, having dissolved the light into space, one quite forcefully utters the sound of "HA" twenty-one times. Once the recitation is complete, one simply remains silently within that state for a time.

Meditation 3

In the third method, one goes outdoors. For this practice, the sky should be a clear blue sky. One turns one's back to the sun and directly gazes at the space without blinking one's eyes. One imagines that the space outside is merged with one's internal space. The space outside and one's mind become completely indivisible. The mind is almost reaching out to the space and the space is completely merged with one's mind. Then one remains in that state for a time.

Those are fundamental meditation practices to cultivate the integration of bliss, luminosity, and non-conceptuality. Without having experiences of this nature, it is almost impossible to experience one's basic being. We can very often think that we are experiencing bliss when we are actually generating desire, and we can think we are generating luminosity when we are actually becoming agitated. These practices are done so we avoid some of these pitfalls.

Experiential Attunement

When one has developed some understanding through meditation, "nyam" begins to manifest. Nyam is a very technical word that is used in both Dzogchen and *Mahamudra*[22] practice, it is not normally used in other practices. Sometimes people translate nyam as "simple understanding," but I do not think that is adequate. Nyam describes both the feeling-tone that is involved, as well as the cognitive process.

I prefer to translate nyam as "experiential attunement." Nyam is related with what has been discussed—non-conceptuality of bliss and non-conceptuality of clarity. One would have all kinds of experiences relating to this. When one has nyam, it is not just a simple process that is taking place in the cortex, but an overall sensation of realization in the body. So, one is attuned to whatever one is experiencing; there is a sense of understanding which is not overly orientated to concepts, and at the same time one has physical sensation involved. As discussed in the previous chapter on union, there are practices designed specifically to develop a particular nyam that one has not been able to attain. Even if one has had experience of nyam in relation to bliss and emptiness, one may not have had the same experience in relation to the others, such as luminosity. Therefore, there are different practices designed to develop the range different types of nyam. For example, in the case of bliss and emptiness, one can engage in the deity yoga practice of *Vajrayogini*[23], the *karmamudra* practice of sexual union, or tummo, the practice of inner heat, which has already been described.

Other practices are done in order to develop the other forms of unity. All these practices are designed to break out of our conventional, habitual way of understanding things. Even though the importance of the practices cannot be underestimated, nonetheless, one may not have to engage in them in order to have nyam. If one engages in Dzogchen practice, without deliberately trying to develop the different nyam through the kinds of practices mentioned, one can have a spontaneous experience of nyam. The practitioner is mainly attempting to achieve experience of nyam in terms of non-duality.

To know if one is experiencing nyam, examples are given in relation to the non-conceptuality of bliss and clarity.

In relation to bliss, one could have the feeling of doing something out of the ordinary, seeming a bit crazy. One could also have extreme emotional experiences that are very dramatic. One may have a very clear sense of what is happening in one's mind but at the same time there is tremendous emotional turmoil manifesting. One might think one's meditation is getting worse or one's emotions are getting more agitated. However, it is not the usual type of emotional drama, as one can see what is actually happening.

In relation to the non-conceptuality of clarity, it is said one would have more predilection towards visual images. Even if you close your eyes, you can see different patterns in front of you. You might have visual images of smoke, mirage like images, and so on. Even if your eyes are open, still you might have visual images of all kinds superimposed onto the object that you are looking at. You might hear things where there is no corresponding sound happening. In the absence of apprehendable sense objects, one's senses still operate in varieties of ways. That is regarded as nyam of clarity.

These experiences are described so if the experiences manifest, the practitioner does not become concerned. When one knows those experiences can happen, and they are not either good or bad, it can be understood as part of the natural process. Once one has understanding, then nyam is the natural outcome and part of the whole process of doing meditation. Therefore, these experiences should be regarded as nyam and not as an obstacle or problem that one has to work with. One just has to let those experiences be, and not entertain them, or make a big deal out of them. They are just indicators or signposts that one is having a momentary experience of Dzogchen.

Chapter Nine

Transcending Self-Image, and the Authentication of Body, Speech, and Mind

Transcendence of the Self-Image

Usually, we have a particular understanding about ourselves, and have a feeling that we are separate from others, as well as from the environment. Such an understanding is based upon notions such as feeling that whatever is outside of me is not me. Therefore, they must be separate from me, because there is some kind of boundary situation. Then there is the notion of autonomy, that is, whatever is within me is under my own control. In other words it is voluntary—I can raise my arms whenever I wish to, I can raise my voice if I wish, I can go and have a cup of tea if I so wish. We have developed varieties of attitudes about ourselves that make us feel that we are somewhat autonomous, and therefore quite separate from others.

However, when we start to look at ourselves closely, we begin to realize that may not be the case. Sometimes we identify ourselves with things that are outside us, such as our possessions, but they can become as if they are part of us. For example, if our possessions get affected, we can feel as though we ourselves are affected. If we lose our possessions, then we could feel that part of ourselves is lost. This can extend to our relationship with others too. When a relationship comes to an end, we can feel as if part of ourselves is gone too, and we may feel it can never be recovered.

Then, when we start to look into our concept of autonomy, we can begin to realize that there are a number of things that go on inside us that we have no control over. For example, our heartbeat— we have absolutely no control over many of the physical processes that go on within ourselves. We don't decide to have a headache but we may get one nonetheless, and we sneeze without meaning to.

The ideas we use to define our identity are only rudimentary, or incidental. They are not essential as a definition of ourselves as a separate entity. All the different attitudes we have developed about ourselves as a separate human being can be seen as based on belief. That belief is a concept that has to be overcome. In the Tibetan system, there is a particular practice that can assist. This practice basically involves giving one's sense of self up, and giving oneself away.

Meditation

Before doing this particular practice, we begin with a breathing and recitation exercise. In this exercise we repeat the sounds "HA" and "HUNG" seven times.

One sits in the meditative posture, breathes in, then repeats "HA-A-A," seven times in an extended way. Take breaths as one needs to through the recitation. Again, one takes another breath in and repeats "HUNG" seven times. This is also repeated as an extended "HU-U-UNG" sound. Then to end this exercise you say "PHAT" once, loudly, and with force. Then remain seated in that particular state, without thinking, visualizing, or contemplating anything, just remaining in one's own natural state. PHAT is usually used as a device to stop one's train of thought, so that one is completely brought to a halt and can more easily remain in one's natural state.

Then you continue with the meditation practice of giving oneself away.

Meditation

Sitting in the meditation posture, one visualizes a situation where there are varieties of beings flocking around you. They want to take parts of you for themselves—aspects of your physicality, intelligence, and so on. How this is experienced and visualized will vary between individuals. Your visualization may take the form of them ripping parts of you away with tremendous aggression, as if they believe that those parts of yourself belong to them. Others come requesting things from you with enormous discretion and courtesy, asking your permission and you giving it to them freely. In the visualization, those beings then leave feeling extremely satisfied, happy, and content.

One does this practice to challenge the many dualistic notions we hold about ourselves—such only being healthy is good, and being unhealthy is bad; being attractive is good, being unattractive is bad; being intelligent is good, being unintelligent is bad, and so on. We no longer seek to view ourselves from that particular perspective. Our whole attitude towards ourselves needs to be completely revolutionized. To do that, we need to let go of our own self-image by completely giving ourselves away, and letting others do whatever they wish with our body and mind.

The Three Gates—Body, Speech, and Mind

The term "the three gates" refers to body, speech, and mind in Buddhism. In Hinayana, the emphasis is placed on the body, which is to say that observance of one's physical behavior is much more important than observance of one's motive. A lot of the emphasis has been placed in relation to how one sits, how one's meditation posture is held, and so on.

In the tantric system, the emphasis is placed on speech. That does not mean speech only in relation to verbalization, but also in relation to our emotions. A lot of our communication is based upon our emotional feelings, moods, and varieties of value judgments. These manifest as speech. Therefore, in Tantra, what the person has to do is not necessarily try to change or modify their behavior, but rather try to understand how their passions come about. How do emotions arise and what are the connections that exist between emotions, passions, and communication.

The tantric practitioner tries to make a proper assessment of their emotions and passions in relation to verbalization, because it is believed that all our emotional experiences are related with communication, and interaction with others. Therefore, tantric techniques such as visualization and mantra recitation are designed to authenticate our speech. Due to this emphasis, mantra recitation is emphasized. There are also varieties of visualization practices, and each deals with a particular emotion. If one is dealing with anger, then a very angry deity, or *Heruka*[24], is visualized. If one has a particular problem with desire, then one visualizes a deity such as Vajrayogini.

In the tantric system, as well as other Buddhist systems, it is understood that our passions normally manifest as destructive and can hinder our communication rather than enhancing it. The reason is our lack clarity, so we use the practices to work on such a problem. All our emotional conflicts and problems with the passions do not arise from the passions and emotions themselves. Rather, it is our lack of understanding, and being unable to make proper assessments of what our emotions comprise of, and how they can be used to improve our understanding of ourselves and others.

With the Dzogchen approach, one is no longer simply concerned with the aspect of communication, but one is more interested in self-knowledge, of understanding one's own true condition, and understanding how things are in reality. The

Dzogchen approach is called "the approach of unconditional." Normally, whenever we enter into a spiritual discipline, our whole orientation is towards self-improvement, either through behavioral modification or adjustment. In contrast, the Dzogchen orientation is towards letting things be without interference, rather than trying to improve or transform them, or bring about particular types of changes.

There is a Tibetan expression that has been used repeatedly in Dzogchen teaching, *nyug mar lhug par zhag*, which means, "simply let everything rest in their true, unconditional state." We interfere with the dynamic processes of the world, and we interfere with our own processes and developments because of our pre-established, pre-conceived ideas. We often view situations as unsatisfactory and feel they should be improved and changed. We start to look at ourselves in the same manner. In Dzogchen, it is said that if we become too preoccupied with the sense of perfecting ourselves, we start to create a split in ourselves. We create an image of ourselves, that which we believe we currently are, and an image that we aspire to that includes all the attributes we believe we are currently lacking. This division creates many unnecessary problems.

Therefore, in Dzogchen, it is said that one has to be able to be oneself for a change. When we start to just simply let ourselves be, instead of interfering with ourselves, we can begin to see a variety of new aspects of ourselves. Aspects not noticed before, and this is true also in relation to how we see and experience the external world. When we start to let things be, we begin to understand more and more how things really are without our interpretations and extrapolations. When we categorize less, we label things less as well, so we begin to have a clearer idea of how things truly exist. We begin to understand the true nature of things. That is why the Dzogchen approach is also called "self-liberation."

If we allow our emotions to manifest, observe them, and simply let go of them, we begin to realize emotions do not need to become a problem. When we resist or do not want to feel different emotions arising, we begin a process of freezing time. As a result of this process of resistance, emotion can intensify simply based on our attitude towards them. When we start to let the emotions just simply be, then the emotions begin to dissipate by themselves quite naturally. Emotions arise by themselves and dissipate by themselves; we do not need to interfere.

The reason why we feel that we should be interfering, that we should be doing this or that, is because we feel that we know implicitly what is good for us, bad for us, what is threatening to us, and not threatening to us. Actually, we do not have a clear idea of what is threatening or non-threatening at all. Therefore, we need to look at ourselves with a fresh perspective. We have been believing some emotions are bad and should be discarded, and others are good and therefore should be developed. We operated that way for a long time and normally without much success. With a fresh perspective, we can really investigate to see if we have implicit knowledge about what is good and bad for us or not. Such a radical change in our attitude gives us an opportunity to view things differently.

According to Dzogchen, what is encouraged is to be able to grasp or experience our transcendental dimension of consciousness. Once we begin to do that, then to talk about renunciation or transformation would lose its potency. As far as the transcendental dimension of one's consciousness is concerned, there is no such thing as negative or positive. There is no such thing as positive karmic traces and dispositions, or negative karmic traces and dispositions—it is completely neutral in that sense. Through such experience, we are more able to adopt a completely different attitude. Therefore, the transcendental aspect is at the forefront of Dzogchen practice. In that way, according to the Dzogchen tradition, we begin to have a completely different understanding of what our body is, what our mind is, and the unity of the body and mind is recognized as being very important.

In the context of Dzogchen, the integration of "being and experience" is important. "Being" refers to the body, and "experience" refers to the mind, or rigpa. The body is not underplayed or demeaned as if our spiritual essence is elsewhere, but currently entrapped in our physical body. From the Dzogchen perspective, it is seen differently. When we begin to establish a more intimate relationship with our body, we have a completely different experience of it, and that is where the notion of Vajra being comes in. "Vajra" normally means "indestructibleness," but what it fundamentally means in this context is that we begin to understand the body as an embodied being. The body is completely saturated with one's transcendental dimension of consciousness and so is no longer just an ordinary body. The body becomes what is known as *ku* in Tibetan, whereas the ordinary body is known as *lu*. Along with that is rigpa, or awareness, which is an inseparable aspect of the body—one cannot be aware unless there is a body that is acting as the basis for it.

Awareness in this particular context is not awareness as we normally understand—that you can be aware that somebody is angry, or you can be aware that there is a tree in the garden. Awareness in this particular case has some sense of immediacy. For example, it is something like, you go out and stub your toe and you go, "Ouch!" It is immediate and it hits you right in the face. In a similar way, the kind of awareness that is talked about here is total awareness of one's own being and one's transcendental aspect of consciousness, free from any judgments, concepts, and conditioning. It is an awareness that does not depend upon learning. It has nothing to do with what we have accumulated so far as a human being in this lifetime or previous lifetimes. It is totally fresh and lucid.

When we begin to understand in that way, we realize all our emotions, thought processes, conditioning, and karmic dispositions, are part of our normal consciousness, they are not part of the transcendental aspect of the consciousness. Therefore, we are not bound by any of it. In a way, our actions are normally quite predetermined. We can't help doing the kinds of things we do because we have accumulated so much karma, we have this enormous karmic reservoir, and are propelled by that. When we begin to realize and experience the transcendental aspect, we realize that it is not really part of our ordinary consciousness. The possibilities of exercising freedom then become a reality. Freedom is not part of our ordinary consciousness, it is part of the transcendental aspect. Here we can see the importance of the notion of self-liberation, rang drol in Tibetan, because in the transcendental region, karma, our conditioning, thought processes, et cetera have no hold whatsoever.

The way to approach this is first, to be able to look at our own ordinary consciousness and ordinary experiences, and then go through that and try to enter into the transcendental aspect. If we look at our ordinary experience, normally our consciousness has this tendency to make things correct and ignore any kind of contingency and unpredictability. It tries to make a very neat world that is safe. But it is not safe. There is nothing that is certain or can be ensured. The world is full of contingencies and we can never guarantee anything. Death is an example. We can die today, tomorrow, anytime—there is no predictability there. Our car can break down, there are all kind of other possibilities to do with relationships, family situations, and so on. They are full of contingencies but we are always trying to make those things solid, real, and non-contingent, to avoid facing such pervasive unpredictability.

However, once we begin to see the contingency in situations and experiences, then we begin to realize that in itself, it is not a bad thing, because contingency within situations makes possible our ability to express freedom. We constantly have to make decisions and choices due to unpredictability. As things are constantly in a state of flux, we are constantly faced with dilemmas of all kinds, so we always have to make a choice—what should we do, how should we act, what is the right move to make. Situations arise because everything is not predetermined, solid, and predictable. If everything happens in a linear way, we would not have to make any choices. Even if you wanted to make a choice, it would not make any difference, because everything would already be predetermined.

Therefore, instead of seeing contingency as something to fear and trying to ignore it, as if it does not exist, and everything is predictable, if we really immerse ourselves into the unpredictability of things, we begin to see the possibility of exercising freedom. That in itself can be something of a problem for us, because when we begin to see that, we can have so much freedom. Then we have to make choices, and making choices means that we have many options and alternatives, and that can create anxiety. However, anxiety, from this particular perspective, is not seen as something bad that we should try to flee from. Rather, it is something that is intrinsic to us when we are exercising our freedom. We have to take responsibility. Taking responsibility means to acknowledge that one has choice and acknowledge that the world is full of contingency. We could believe that responsibility is normally equated with taking blame—if we take responsibility, we need to be willing to say we have been wrong and someone else has been right. However, here responsibility means we are willing to face up to our own decisions and choices. That does not mean one needs to be put into the wrong and the other person in the right. That type of conditioning is part of the ordinary consciousness and not the transcendental domain of the consciousness.

As one resides more in the transcendental aspect, all of the emotional problems and karmic conflicts are transcended, or become self-liberated. That is precisely what rang drol means. It also means that the person is not released from the samsaric situation by somebody else, by a Buddha, teacher, or guru to reach enlightenment, but it is done by the person themselves. Liberation or freedom comes about because it is an intrinsic part of transcendental consciousness. Therefore, we are already free. To talk about "freedom from something" is in contradiction to the Dzogchen way of thinking. One does not get freed from anything.

Freedom is seen to be something that is intrinsic to oneself. When we begin to look at the workings of the mind and body through meditation, gradually we see how this is possible. We begin to see that we have a transcendental dimension, and are not confined to experiences of certain negative emotions, habitual thought processes, et cetera but there is another aspect to oneself. This view is extremely important within the Dzogchen way of thinking.

Having discussed the sense of freedom that accompanies the realization of one's transcendental aspect of the consciousness, we come to the other aspect of being, the body. As discussed earlier the body is often regarded as something basic and trivial, or even seen as a nuisance in the attainment of spiritual realization. The body is intimately related, not only with our consciousness, but even with transcendental consciousness. Once we begin to experience the body properly, then the body itself has a transcendental aspect to it, and we begin to become much more in tune with the way the body operates.

As mentioned, the ordinary way we experience the body is called lus in Tibetan, and the transcendental aspect of the body is called sku. The Dzogchen teachings in particular consider this distinction very important. The body is wrapped in karmic traces and dispositions, as is the mind. The body has a tendency to operate in a predictable and habituated way. Through meditation, one can free oneself from these particular ways of acting and behaving. This is extremely important, because the body provides the opportunity for encounters, communication, and other interactions. We know others by their behavior and expressions. By observing them and their behavior, we begin to make assessments of them. We know if they are angry or happy, sad or agitated, et cetera. Interrelationships with other human beings are expressed through the body.

Our expression of compassion and love are other mediums that we try to communicate with others, which are also done through our body. Therefore, without the body, and having a good understanding of body, we can misuse it. That can only diminish our capacity to communicate, relate to others. Without a good understanding of body, it will be in a state of disarray, disorganized, and our emotions and thoughts would also be agitated and in disarray. Through integrating one's experience of body and emotions through meditating, one can see how the body and mind are intimately related, and how experiencing the body properly leads us to a completely new understanding of the body. Therefore, we have to pay as much attention to the body as we pay attention to the mind.

Karma literally means "action," and it is through the body that we act. One can have an intention to act, but without using the body, the act would not be accomplished, in fact, it would not be able to be initiated. If you are to bring an act into fruition, you have to use your limbs and your body. Once we begin to pay attention to all this, then we can see how we are karmically habituated to act in different ways. In mentally ill people, it becomes very apparent that this karmic thing can go overboard. Some obsessive-compulsive patients have to wash their hands twenty times per day or more, others have to repeatedly clean out their cupboards day in day out. You can tell them to relax and not worry about it but the person has some excuse for doing it again and again. In fact, when we begin to look at ourselves and how we behave, we see some similarities to these extreme examples. This is extremely important, as that is an expression of the body, so one has to have proper understanding of that. Even enlightened beings have a body in order to be with normal beings, to communicate and work with them. However, enlightened beings' understanding of the body would be slightly different.

There are a methods in Dzogchen one can practice in order to break away from one's conventional way of behaving.

Meditation

Find a private place. Go to an empty place, or lock yourself up in your room, and act out whatever you want to act out. If you want to scream, or act like a dog, or do anything you want to do, you act it out.

The reason why this exercise is done is to allow oneself to initiate actions that we refrained from because of so many assumptions, presuppositions, and social conditions that have been introduced to us, so we are acting out whatever we want in a non-harming way within this exercise. With this Dzogchen method, one is "acting out" yet also being very aware. There should be no one to see what is happening, what you are going through, to observe what you are doing, to interpret your behavior. You are the observer and the observed, you are the spectator as well as the performer, and you are doing whatever you want to do and you are doing that with awareness. One can then begin to observe completely different states of mind when acting out. It is an opportunity to see how our mind operates, how our body operates, and how our behavior affects our states of mind. We begin to realize the intimate relationship between body and mind.

You should exhaust yourself by acting out in this manner and then when you have exhausted yourself, you just let be. There is a Dzogchen technical term *nalmar naspa*, in Tibetan. *Nalmar* means "state of naturalness," and *naspa* means "exist"—so, existing in the state of naturalness. Because your body is relaxed, all the muscles are tired out, so your body is relaxed and your mind begins to stop chattering as well, and you rest in that natural state. You don't have to sit upright; you can just lie down and just be in the natural state. That is one kind of method.

Another method more conventional in Buddhist terms involves visualization, however in Dzogchen, visualization is not done with deities or mandalas. The Dzogchen tradition does not have any iconography so here there are no images of deities though some mantras are used. The visualization is a technique to bring one's body up—to reveal, be in sync with, or empathize with one's body. In doing so, one begins to understand the transcendental dimension of the body and sees one's body as sku, not as a lus. We should say "feeling it as sku." It has more to do with feeling-tone than an intellectual process. One has to sense one's body and elevate it from its normal existence into a high level of being known as the "vajra body," *dorje sku* in Tibetan. Dorje is vajra and sku is understood as transcendental. Once we begin to do that, we also begin to see the connection between body, speech, and mind.

Another way of interacting and communicating with other human beings is speech. Besides sign language and using our limbs, we speak, and speech comes from the body. Without body, there would be no speech. Speech is intimately related with one's body. In conventional tantric literature, it is said that speech is connected with *prana*. Prana literally means "breath," but it also means much more than breath. Articulation of speech comes about because of prana. Prana resides in the body, and body and speech are intimately related.

Then there is the mind. Mind cannot be separated from speech and the body. Mind that cannot be articulated, that cannot instigate action, is no mind at all, it is completely impotent, there is no consciousness whatsoever. Therefore, these three principles of body, speech, and mind are intimately related. When fully integrated, they are known as the "three principles of vajra"—vajra body, vajra mind, and vajra speech. The epithet vajra is used to denote the unshakability. The profundity of this relationship denotes speech is much more than verbalization. If we begin to look at that more closely, we can see speech can be used or misused depending on how well we are understanding ourselves, and how we relate to our transcendental aspect. So those three things are involved there.

In another visualization method, you visualize three syllables. The first one is OM, the second one is AH, and the third one is HUNG. OM is white, AH is red, and HUNG is blue, and they correspond to the elevated aspects, or transcendental aspects, of body, speech, and mind. The vajra body, vajra speech, and vajra mind that constitute our being are visualized to decondition and free ourselves of habits and habitual processes formed by our environment and psychological make up that create certain tendencies to beliefs. These dispositions come about because of internal and external causes. The internal causes are the classic Buddhist emotional afflictions of desire, aggression, jealously, pride, and ignorance.

With this visualization, you use your body as centers of your emotional afflictions. Pride and jealousy are especially located in the head region. Desire is located in the navel region, and ignorance, greed, and anger in the lower part of the abdominal region. There is a reason why they are ordered that way. When a person is proud, there is a sense of upliftedness, an upward kind of feeling. Desire is located in the middle region, and greed and anger are seen as very basic earthy types of emotions and they are located in the lower part of the body.

Meditation

Sitting in the meditation posture, first rest the mind for a time to settle it. When you are ready, you can begin the meditation.

Visualize the syllable OM in the head center, AH in the throat center, and HUNG in the navel center. OM radiates white light and it pushes the neurosis of pride and jealously downwards. At the throat, red light radiates and it pushes the desire downwards. HUNG radiates blue light and it pushes the anger and greed downwards, and they are washed out of your body through your feet. This process is repeated and it is said that you should spend more time as you approach the feet, and that is because the anger, greed, and ignorance need to be worked with more. So that can be done repeatedly.

Once one has finished doing that for a time, then one should try to feel the body as it is, without any conception, without any judgment, and try to be in a pre-reflective state of mind, which is the transcendental consciousness. Just be, which is nalmar naspa, as mentioned previously. That means to just be in the natural state and not condition it. Avoid thinking about things or judging any thoughts that arise. At the same time, feel the body completely and try to expand your consciousness so the consciousness envelopes the body, instead of the body acting as a machine of the ordinary consciousness.

The classic western paradigm of the interaction between body and mind is called "ghost in the machine theory."[25] The ghost is exorcised through this mantra, then one has to expand one's consciousness, and the consciousness begins to pervade every single part of one's body. It goes right through one's bone and marrow, and one's body and consciousness become completely inseparable, and one just rests in that state. By doing that, one is using a particular method to decondition oneself, to see things differently, to introduce a new viewpoint.

Authentication of Body, Speech, and Mind

In the Buddhist tradition generally, and in Tantra and Dzogchen in particular, the authentication of the three gates, body, speech, and mind is considered to be extremely important. Sometimes it is called "mixing of the three gates." It means that usually, physical actions, mental attitudes of motive, and the way in which we utter speech are incongruent; they are not complementary with each other. It also means that ordinarily we have alienated ourselves from our body and our capacity to be able to speak, and our mental experiences. So the integration, or the mixing of the three gates, involves engagement rather than disengagement, whereby we disengage ourselves from our body or from our speech. For instance, sometimes our mental attitude does not comply with our actions; sometimes what we are thinking and what we say become incongruent. There can be a conflict between body, speech, and mind, which has already been approached to some degree in the being and experience discussion earlier in the book.

We may have a body and feel we own it; having the capacity to be able to talk is seen as something that we own or possess. The capacity to be able to think is also seen in this way. The separation between the *owner* and the *owned* denotes our attitudes all the time. The integration of body, speech, and mind involves overcoming the idea of ownership. Instead of seeing our body, speech, and mind as possessions, we become intimately involved with the three so we begin to become indistinguishable from them, and as a result, we cease to be their owners. We become our body, we become our speech, we become our mind, which is an extremely difficult position to maintain when you are living in a dualistic condition.

When we begin to integrate our body, speech, and mind, we are transcending our broader dualist condition simultaneously. The separation between the actor and the act, the speaker and the speech, the thinker and the thought, become completely united and identical.

To have a body, the capacity to use language, and a mind that can think, reason, and have experiences of all kinds is part of our human capability. Even though we have such capacity through the three gates, we are unable to make proper use of them within our ordinary circumstances. When we are thinking in terms of our body, we become either overly obsessed with how we look, what we eat, and so on, or we choose the other extreme and ignore the body's requirements. In both approaches, there is a sense of disownment. That is, the body is something that one has rather than something that one is. The body ceases to be a lived body. It almost becomes an inanimate object.

Integration with one's body, is called "realization of the vajra body," distinguished from our ordinary experience of the body. Realization of the vajra body is achieved through a variety of yogic exercises, such as the Vajra posture which I mentioned earlier. Yogic exercises are not designed purely for physical fitness or purely for health reasons. These reasons are important, but the primary reason is to come into proper contact with one's body. The body becomes oneself, and oneself is the body, rather than one possessing the body as one would possess property or a car.

The second is "authentication of speech." The authenticated version of speech is called "vajra speech," as opposed to our normal verbal communications. The reason it is called authentic speech, or vajra speech is because we are normally talking without fully understanding what we are speaking about, and without the presence of rigpa, or bare awareness. There is an absolute lack of bare awareness when we are engaging in speech. This lack of awareness in our speech produces gibberish and confusion and dissociation from our own experience. When we talk, we normally avoid fully experiencing. Verbalizing about our problem, or gossiping about others helps avoid experiencing things directly. We can preferably let ourselves simply be and experience ourselves just as we are. In that way, we can provide the opportunity to overcome the concealment of our own being, and allow it to reveal itself.

We need to authenticate our speech so it becomes part of ourselves, rather than using speech as an instrument of manipulation. Gossip is an example of the inauthenticity of speech. There are a number of ways to use damaging words—verbalized or written—where the composition of stories is designed to hurt, disguise, or defame.

There are varieties of ways we engage in inauthenticity with our body, speech, and mind creating incongruities with these three gates. In relation to the mind, it is seen as the instigator of all other avenues of inauthenticity, caused by over-conceptualization, or vikalpa. The more we conceptualize, the more we become dissociated from our body and misuse our speech. So our human activities will normally lack authenticity and awareness and it is this incongruity of the three gates that the Dzogchen and tantric practices try to rectify.

Ascetic practices are also a way of dealing with the body. These practices can lead to dissociation from one's body, rather than association. It can become a process of disengagement from the body and oneself, rather than engagement to oneself. The ascetic may see the body as just a bag of flesh and blood, to be dispossessed. All manner of disassociations need to be rectified.

There are certain exercises related with the authentication of body, speech, and mind. By engaging in these exercises, the practitioner is trying to become completely exhausted, absorbed, or possessed by the practice in order to forget to conceptualize. When we forget to conceptualize, we begin to gain more insight into our way of being. We begin to simply be with ourselves—our body, speech, and mind.

Vajra Posture Practice

The Vajra posture is a strenuous isometric posture designed to push body and mind into a state of beneficial stress. Caution should be practiced by anyone with physical ailments.[26]

One begins this practice by sitting in meditation for a short period. One then rises and assumes the Vajra posture—by standing tensed with heels together and the knees bent and stretched out to the sides. The spine should be straight and the palms placed together over the crown of the head. The chin is pulled towards the larynx, and the eyes open and looking straight ahead. One can visualize either a white AH, or a white translucent ball, below the navel, and focus one's awareness there. One observes the flow of energy and sensation within the body while pushing through the barriers of pain and exhaustion. One maintains this position for as long as one is possibly able to until the body can no longer hold this position. One then collapses to the ground and completely relaxes for a brief time. Then one resumes the sitting meditation position with eyes open looking directly ahead, and remains in a completely relaxed, open manner, not concentrating or fixating on anything. The same process should then be repeated at will.

AH Practice

With this practice, we are trying to bring our body, speech, and mind into harmony and concordance. The practice involves simply repeating one syllable, AH. This syllable AH is considered extraordinarily important in Dzogchen. Its importance lies in the very seemingly simple nature of the utterance. The reason that is the case is that according to Dzogchen, AH is the origin of all sounds. Without the utterance of AH, one would not be able to articulate any sound at all. As it is the origin of the sound, one could say it is the origin of all mantras. Usually mantras are inarticulate, they don't mean anything. The very reason why the mantras become powerful is not because of what they say or that they make sense, but because of the fact that mantras are all about primitive sound—the basic, original, primordial sound.

Meditation

One sits in normal meditation position, relaxes for a brief time, then utters AH slowly, and then continues to repeat it while remaining aware of the sound, and the vibration in the throat. The mind should concentrate on the throat and the sound. With the body, when one utters AH, one remains aware of the activity of the chest, and abdomen, and feels the vibration in the throat. While repeating AH, we imagine that all our concepts, ideas, personal history—educational background, occupations, family background, all kinds of ideas and concepts that we have about ourselves, who we are, what we are—simply dissolve. All ideas about our identity dissolve together. As the sound of AH dissolves, simultaneously all our concepts and ideas et cetera dissolve too. We repeat this visualization about twenty-five times, then we sit in the normal meditation posture, and return to Dzogchen practice—with a sense of spaciousness and non-duality, letting the mind be as it is. If you are doing a longer meditation session, then you can repeat this another twenty times before returning to the Dzogchen practice before finishing the session.

HUNG Practice

HUNG practice also involves the integration of body, speech, and mind. The reason why you just simply utter HUNG instead of saying a particular sentence or something like that is because all articulate sound is produced out of an inarticulate sound. All the speech, the capacity to be able to structure sentences, and so on, is a product of the original sound, which is totally inarticulate. When you say Hung, that is not an articulate sound. When you begin to do this practice, you have a sense of posture, which deals with your body, and your body is postured in such a way that you can't help but to notice it and to dwell in your body. The sound is produced in such a way that it brings about some kind of physical reaction, so that the body responds when you utter that particular sound. It is not like our ordinary speech where the speech doesn't really put as much effect on the body at all. The mind is also brought back from its fantasies to the moment that you are living in, back to the present.

Therefore, there is the conjunction of the correlation of body, speech, and mind taking place all at once, in the one moment. All three of them are activated in that particular short moment, and one's experience of the three is also taking place in that very moment, which is not the case in our ordinary life.

Meditation

One sits in the normal meditation position. In this particular case, one has their arms stretched down completely straight. The fingers are rolled over the thumbs but not clenched. The back of the hands sit on top of the thighs, against the abdomen, and the arms are flexed and push the shoulders upward. It is said that the shoulders should look like a lion about to pounce on its prey. The chest should be extended and protruding. Instead of gazing down with half-closed eyes as is often prescribed, one looks straight ahead and slightly upwards so the eyes are completely open as if you are glaring at something. Then breathe in and as you breath out—with an extended out breath—utter "HUNG." Continue this rhythm of reciting "HUNG" with each extended out breath. When saying "HUNG," allow all concepts and ideas to simply dissipate. The energy of the sound itself can dissipate our ordinary trivial thoughts. Then broadening our awareness, we continue to repeat the "HUNG" recitation, and also concentrate on our physical posture as well as the sound of "HUNG", and also include an awareness of the sensations within our vocal chords. With one's gaze, we continue to simply look at, or fixate on whatever is in our direct line of vision.

In the process of authenticating body, speech, and mind, one can have portentous dreams that suggest the person's level of realization and understanding. Indicating the authentication of one's body can result in different kinds of physical reactions, and manifestations may take place, such as trembling. One may feel they are suffering from fever or feel jittery. With authentication of speech, one may spontaneously laugh or make inarticulate noises. Indicating authentication of mind, irrespective of what is going on in one's mind, the person is able to remain aware and remain with the experience. These are considered classic signs of authentication of one's body, speech, and mind.

Presence of Numen

The "presence of numen," *dag nang* in Tibetan, can also be translated as "sacred outlook," or "purity perception." I believe the "presence of numen," is a more appropriate translation. "Numen" has the connotation of something spiritual and quite mysterious at the same time. It means something similar to "awe-inspiring," "spiritual," "mysterious," and even "divine."

As one begins to practice the authentication of body, speech, and mind, gradually one will have varieties of nyam, experiential attunements. We then begin to become more aware of our fundamental, existential way of being. As a result, we understand the limitations of conceptual frames of reference, seeing all experience and existence in the context of the ground of being. This is why it is called "presence of numen," "purity perception," or "sacred outlook."

One's outlook becomes sacred when one sees the phenomenal world from a different perspective, when there is a total shift of one's conceptual apparatus, when one's sensory perceptions are no longer bound by conceptual frames of reference. Each individual is usually trapped within their own mind and it is difficult to shift one's conceptual apparatus to be able to perceive things in a direct way.

When we are able to overcome the third order of reality, the notional-conceptual or conceptual frame of reference, one is able to see the second order of reality within the context of the ground of being which is the first order of reality. Therefore, whatever we perceive becomes something spiritual, something divine. It is said that one is able to see the world as a divine mansion, a metaphor that should not be taken literally. For example, if we are able to see a tree not only as a tree, but also as a tree that is inseparable from the reality, meaning the way the tree truly and genuinely exists, this cannot be done if we are bound by our own conceptual frame of reference.

Based upon that premise, one can establish a proper relationship with other human beings on a much more genuine basis. The reason is that one is no longer biased in relation to one's perception of others. Perhaps the expression that the Jewish existentialist Martin Buber[27] used is appropriate, the "I-Thou relationship." Usually, when we relate to each other, it is an "I-It relationship." What I believe Buber meant was, there is no real existential commitment in relation to other people. We try to reduce the other person to something "thing-like." We relate to other people as we relate to our possessions—our cars, furniture, house, property, and so on. There is a tremendous sense of attachment, possessiveness, and selfishness, but very little appreciation of the uniqueness of the other person. Therefore, the relationship is I-It rather than what he called I-Thou.

When one begins to overcome the conceptual frame of reference, one begins to see the possibility of relating to the other person as "thou" rather than as an "it." One is no longer trying to fit the other person into a particular model of what one thinks the other person should be like. Instead, one is able to appreciate the person for what they are. That is why the relationship becomes I-Thou instead of I-It.

In the context of the I-Thou relationship, one is not just simply trying to assess the other person intellectually, but one begins to communicate with the other person in terms of one's feelings and emotions in varieties of ways. One can communicate on an extra-verbal level, if you like. One's communication with others is not simply based on verbalization.

Usually, when we say, "We should communicate with each other," it indicates the assumption that a proper relationship is based upon communication, that if we have any problems, we should talk it out. This is arguably a present-day cliché of what communication is largely based upon, a model of technology and the sharing of information. When we talk about communication in this way, it is based on an exchange of information rather than a sense of existential communication.

In the I-Thou relationship, one goes beyond sharing information and verbal interchange. Communicating in this way can become based on inauthentic speech. Communication in a more spiritual sense is more than seeing a person who has a body and mind, all kinds of problems and neuroses et cetera but the person is seen as a fully developed human being. From the Dzogchen perspective, no matter how corrupt and neurotic someone may appear to be, at the same time, their foundation is the ground of being.

In the Buddhist context, it is said that when one begins to view others in this way, we begin to see them as a god or goddess. That is of course just metaphorical. The point is that we never lose sight of the transcendental aspect of a person. They may not be aware of it, they may be completely involved in self-estrangement, be extremely difficult and neurotic, and so forth. Even then, we do not lose sight of the ground of being inherent in that person. The person should be seen from this particular point of view rather than adopting a position of superiority and dealing with other people, and even things, from a disdainful perspective or position.

In other words, the I-Thou relationship is established when one's relationship with oneself becomes authentic in relation to body, speech, and mind. When one's relationship with oneself becomes authentic, one's relationship with others becomes authentic as well. It becomes the I-Thou relationship instead of the I-It relationship. We see the whole person rather than dissecting the person into a bundle of fragmented pieces of personality and attributes. Instead of our incessant analysis of everything in this world, things, and people, we are able to see things in their entirety.

The importance of developing a proper relationship with our body, speech, and mind cannot be emphasized enough. Sometimes when we perform an action, it is as if the action is perpetrated by someone else, and we can feel as if we are not entirely responsible for our actions and their outcomes. In part, one has disowned their body. Until one has re-established an authentic relationship with one's body, speech, and mind, one's relationship with others cannot be entirely authenticated. Until we have authenticated our body, speech, and mind through developing some of the nyam, the experiential attunements, we are confined to solipsism or autism in some ways. To have an authentic relationship with others, it must begin from oneself. In Dzogchen practice, self-realization or authentic selfhood is the starting point of any kind of interpersonal relationship.

Chapter Ten

Imagination and the Five Elements and the Four Modes of Resting in Meditation

Having discussed the authentication of the body and speech in some detail, we will now look into working with the mind in relation to the imagination and the five elements. Most of the time, we are strangers to ourselves and may know little about our own human condition. As we are already alienated from ourselves, to be able to establish a proper relationship with others and the world becomes extremely difficult and precarious. All kinds of anxieties develop. We don't have to be crazy or psychotic to have all types of anxieties, due to being disengaged from ourselves and others.

This particular practice can help gain more insight into how one is relating to oneself and what sort of understanding one has of oneself, which is extremely important. People may have a sort of anxiousness where they feel that they should withdraw from others and have nothing to do with them, and as a result, live in some sort of solitude. Or they may feel completely insecure by being by themselves, that the fear of loneliness is too much. There is this fear that one will be engulfed by other people and their socialization, feeling that one will be influenced by others too much, and therefore lose one's own identity and become just like everyone else.

This could be on the social side as well as on the personal side. In terms of family situations, a lot of kids leave home thinking, "I don't want to grow up just like my father," or "I don't want to grow up just like my mother." However, the more they run away thinking that they are different, the more they end up being the same later on.

The basic problem is ambivalence, this ambivalent attitude that we have towards ourselves and towards others. Bearing that in mind, these exercises that are being presented are to make us become more and more in tune with how we feel, what sort of self-perception we have of ourselves, and to try to reassess our situation. Through use of some of these exercises, there is the possibility that even if we have some understanding of what we believe ourselves to be, that may in fact be radically changed. We may reassess ourselves and see ourselves in a completely different light. There is always that possibility.

A lot of the time, our interactions with other human beings, even when it is intended to benefit others, fall short of authenticity. For instance, there is a psychiatric case where a supposedly psychotic woman was given a cup of tea by a nurse and the woman said, "Thank you very, very much. I have never been given a cup of tea." Generally, people wouldn't take any notice of that. They would think, "This crazy woman, she's gibbering away." But this particular psychiatrist realized that what she really meant was that nobody cared for her enough to give her a cup of tea in the way this particular nurse did. A lot of the time, people either gave her a cup of tea out of pity, or whatever it might be, but never in a very genuine sense. The statement that she made was a complete appreciation of the whole thing.

This is true of a lot of our behavior as well. When we give something, even a cup of tea, there could be a lot of things involved. Maybe we want to display our tea set, or maybe we want to show how many varieties of tea we have. The last thing we may have on our mind is to give a proper, genuine cup of tea to the other person. Maybe it's just as a social courtesy, when someone comes into the house you are supposed to offer them some tea. It's part of the ritual, rather than a genuine feeling for the other person, thinking, "I should be offering a cup of tea."

All of those examples are worth thinking about. Those things only indirectly touch on the meditation on the five elements. The meditation on the five elements is done in order to work with the mind by using imagination. We do not realize how much the mind can imagine things and what sort of transformation can take place due to the power of imagination itself. Sometimes people tend to get fantasy and imagination confused and think that they are the same, but they are two totally different things. When you have a fantasy, you can't help but fantasize, you don't decide to fantasize. If that were the case, then it wouldn't be fantasy. With imagination, you deliberately imagine a particular situation. You imagine yourself as being this, or being that, or whatever it might be, whereas with fantasy, it just comes out of nowhere.

Meditations on the Five Elements

There are five meditation practices relating with the five elements of air, fire, water, earth, and space, and these are practiced in consecutive order.

Air

The first one is air, and air is visualized as green. You imagine a situation where you are the only person in a particular place. You visualize yourself in a landscape, it could be a desert or a place that has trees and different foliage, there could be birds singing. You could be sitting on a mountain top and looking out into the horizon. Everything is green. You think that you are in the most peaceful place. There is absolute peace there, tranquility.

Suddenly, a violent, turbulent storm breaks out and begins to destroy everything. You get completely thrown around and everything begins to disintegrate because of the air.

Your body begins to disintegrate, as well as what you might regard yourself to be in terms of karmic dispositions, concepts, ideas, imagination, and memory. Everything is completely destroyed. There is nothing left except this particular witness who is you, with no memory, nothing, but still a sense of the "I am" that was discussed earlier. There is just the basic condition of existence, nothing else. One is stripped of everything except the fact that you simply exist.

Fire

The next one is fire. Again, you visualize yourself in any situation and imagine that everything is peaceful. In this instance though, the environment is red. Your body is red, everything is red, there are no other colors but red. If you are in a forest, all the trees are red, the ground is red, the sky is red. You imagine that it is extraordinarily peaceful to be in that particular situation.

Suddenly, the peace is disrupted by a forest fire. You get caught in the fire and are being consumed by the fire. You see yourself being consumed. It completely destroys your body as well as the mind. All your karmic traces and dispositions, your concepts, ideas, upbringing, if you have hatred towards somebody because of past history, any attachment one may have towards one's relatives or friends, all of that is immediately completely wiped out. It is as if you have gone back to being a baby again, in some ways. You have no traces and dispositions of any sort. Everything is completely consumed by this extraordinary fire.

Water

The next is water. Everything is white. You are in a completely white environment. Whatever you see has the color white. Your body and everything is white. You are feeling extraordinarily comfortable, peaceful, and relaxed, feeling very good.

Then suddenly, a flood begins to come out of nowhere. Everything is completely destroyed, including oneself. Again, one's karmic dispositions and all the rest become completely wiped out. One is just simply there, not as a body, nor as someone who has a past history, but as someone who does not have any past history, who has suddenly become a stranger in the sense that you have no memory or relationship to anyone. It is as if you are in the middle of space with nobody around and you don't even have a body to look at.

Earth

The next is earth, which is yellow. There is a complete sense of yellowness. Everything around you is completely yellow and you are yellow. Again, you feel calm and tranquil. Suddenly, the earth begins to shake. Everything begins to disintegrate, decompose. Again, you are left with nothing.

Space

Eventually, you come to space, which is blue. When you come to space, you simply rest in that state. The imagination of space is when you imagine the space all around you with nothing else. You don't have a body at that moment. When you visualize space, you simply rest in that state. You don't have to think about anything, you don't have to think there is any kind of disruption, you simply continue to stay in that state.

Gradually, you imagine that all the elements come back together and reconstitute themselves.

By doing this practice, one can gradually begin to reconstruct one's view of oneself. There can be some kind of fundamental reorientation and reassessment of one's view of oneself that takes place. Normally, we are so fixated with who we are, what we look like, how we see ourselves, how people see us, and how we see people seeing us, et cetera. Such a construction is complicated. This practice is designed to help deconstruct, so we can reconstitute our identity, to come from a completely different non egocentric angle. That is basically the idea of the practice.

Also, the elements are considered to be fundamental constituents of our body's construct—the breath is air, body heat is fire, body fluid is water, solidity is earth, and the body's cavities are space. Through the five element practice, we seek to deconstruct our concepts of our body as a solid thing and it helps us to recognize the body as insubstantial and less defined.

Four Modes of Resting in Dzogchen Meditation

From the Dzogchen perspective, as we have seen, all the other Buddhist approaches to meditation, visualization, recitation of mantras, and so on, are considered to be working with one's ordinary consciousness. Those approaches do not focus on or work with the fundamental way of being, mind-in-itself, or ground of being. Therefore, those approaches do not focus on rigpa, bare awareness. It is extremely important to remember that when one is doing Dzogchen meditation, one is neither accepting nor rejecting anything, not trying to cultivate healthy states of mind or renounce unhealthy states of mind. Rather, one simply tries to accept oneself as a whole person. When one starts to do the practice in that particular mode, there are four ways in which one can rest one's mind.

Resting One's Mind Like a Mountain

The first mode is called "resting one's mind like a

mountain." What that means is that instead of trying to see whether one is having any thoughts taking place in the mind, or going through any emotional state, one should try to rest simply as it is. When one has developed a certain confidence within oneself, one does not try to pretend to be doing this and that. One does not even think of doing meditation. One can just simply be. That is why the image of the mountain is used. There is a sense of groundedness, a sense of complete majesty. This can come about when the person is becoming less and less ego orientated and more and more rigpa orientated.

Resting One's Mind Like an Ocean

The second mode is called "resting one's mind like an ocean." The image of the ocean is used because no matter how turbulent the sea may be on the surface, at the bottom of the sea, it is always still. In a similar kind of way, no matter what sorts of emotional agitation we may be going through, no matter what sorts of personal changes might be taking place on the surface, fundamentally, as far as the ground of our own being is concerned, nothing of that is happening at all. There is a sense of total stillness. Whenever one is having emotional upheavals during meditation, one can see them as just waves on the ocean. They do not disturb one's basic level of being, and they are unable to corrupt the impeccability of rigpa, or bare awareness.

Resting One's Mind in Bare Awareness

The third mode is called "resting one's mind in bare awareness." What that means is that one should be more concerned in regard to awareness, than what is taking place in one's mind. Whatever is taking place in one's mind should be allowed to be there. There should be no censorship of any kind as to what one is allowed to experience or what one is not allowed to think or experience. There is a total lack of censorship in terms of what one experiences, with bare awareness present. One wants to rest one's mind in bare awareness, a necessary requirement within self-realization.

Resting with the Appearance of Phenomena

The fourth mode is called "resting with the appearance of phenomena." What that means is that in Dzogchen practice, one does not have to turn away from the senses. Usually, when we meditate, it is said that the senses corrupt the meditator because through the senses, we experience pleasure, and the more one is outward directed, in terms of relating to the world through our five senses, the more chance there is of being corrupted and influenced. Therefore, blocking senses is often suggested to keep the mind pure. The idea of "out of sight, out of mind," is being practiced—if one doesn't look at it, nothing will happen. Then hopefully one would be able to gain some kind of spiritual realization as a result of that approach.

In Dzogchen practice, it is viewed and practiced differently. Senses are seen as just senses, and the sense organs just seen as sense organs. The sense fields—visual, auditory, et cetera—are considered inanimate and are not able to incite either pleasure or pain. The reason why we experience pleasure, pain, and other types of experience, is due to our own mind. When our mind fixates and has attachment for certain experiences, it seeks further stimulus, and perpetuation of excitement, resulting in agitation of the mind. The cause is not because of the senses but more so, the way in which the mind apprehends things.

In Dzogchen meditation practice, we can simply look at the visual field and rest with that. That is a meditation in itself. We can listen to a sound and rest with that. One can taste something and simply rest in that particular experience of taste. All the senses can be used as modes to develop a bare awareness as they become a part of meditation. Instead of trying to block our senses, trying not to hear, see, taste, et cetera, it is better to have our senses—eyes and ears et cetera—wide open. It also makes us a more integrated human if the senses are exercised properly.

All of the senses can be used as modes of spiritual practice. As emphasized, the major aim is to develop awareness, bare awareness. As long as there is bare awareness, one does not need to think in terms of renunciation or transformation. By developing awareness, by becoming in touch with rigpa, one gains more insight into oneself, and in many ways is able to break down one's habitual mode of operating.

Chapter Eleven

Actualization of the Ground

In Dzogchen practice the beginning and the end are not separate. The very starting point is the end itself. There is no difference between the *alpha* and *omega*, in the sense that when you realize Dzogchen, you have not realized anything different from what you already possess.

No distinction is made in Dzogchen between the confused state of mind and the enlightened state of mind. The only difference is that of perspective, and perception. When one has estranged oneself from one's true condition, then one is confused, and when one is able to become engaged with oneself again, then one becomes the so-called enlightened person. However, what the person has realized is that they are already there, and this is why it has been said that a person is already enlightened but does not know it—because one is influenced by one's biased way of thinking, and this leads to imbalance.

While we constantly aspire to be balanced and have equilibrium et cetera while being unable to accept different aspects of ourselves—wanting to cultivate different qualities, personality traits we do not believe we possess—we find such an attitude cannot engender balance. Balance is not created by wanting to reject certain things and cultivate others. It is achieved through acceptance of one's condition. That is why in Dzogchen it is said that one should not have to feel neurotic about one's neurosis.

There is a much more sane approach. That is, to be able to be gentle with oneself, with one's neurosis and emotional conflicts. We cannot achieve balance by becoming angry at our anger, by self-condemnation, or by feeling that one is inadequate. It is important to have a positive approach based on accepting oneself as one is. That does not mean that there is a true nature that is hidden behind the way we are. It is the way we are, warts and all. Being able to accept ourselves in that way is the starting point that leads to realization where one begins to experience oneself as a whole person.

When one starts to look at the temporality of one's own true condition, one's own mortality, as well as the temporality of things external to oneself, it does not lead to despair and nihilism. This leads to real pleasure and bliss in the sense that we are no longer afflicted by the idea that we are somehow inadequate. It also brings about a certain particular confidence within oneself, which is different from either arrogance or pride. The self-confidence that is being talked about in Dzogchen is different from what we normally regard as confidence. Usually, we regard confidence as being associated with some particular aspect of ourselves, we feel confident due to a particular reason. Confidence in Dzogchen does not have a particular reason as such. It is unconditional, manifesting because the person is able to accept themselves as they are. Pride and arrogance is conditional and leads to opinionatedness. If a person is fully confident, they are willing to be wrong, and proven wrong, and admonished, and are still able to hold their own ground. A person who is proud and arrogant becomes more and more defensive, aggressive, opinionated, and develops a growing desire to be righteous, and free of doubt and uncertainty.

Due to the development of this unconditional type of confidence, the person starts to have spiritual experience, nyam— the experience of great bliss, or great pleasure, *maha sukha* in

Sanskrit, *dewa chenpo* in Tibetan. With this experience, one is totally open to criticism, rejections, and all kinds of normally unwanted advances from others. This is extremely important. Even intellectually, if a person is confident in oneself, then they are able to listen to other people's opinions, views, and attitudes. However, if a person is not confident, they will want to shut out opposing views, close their eyes and ears, and not want to see or hear that which is outside their area of belief, and this leads to a catatonic position. Lacking a clear confidence, we arrest the opportunity to be in touch with the environment, and in connection with others. Overcoming the duality of subject and object, oneself and others, is achieved through openness, and through self-confidence. When one is truly self-confident in this way, one is able to reach out, and is willing to encompass and engage. When one is not self-confident, then one wants to push away, reject, disengage, and one experiences varieties of disconnections, including alienation and loneliness.

We normally feel self-confidence is based upon some kind of external situation, or developed due to other people's opinions et cetera by acquiring a particular title, position, or stature in society. From the Dzogchen perspective, real self-confidence has to come from within, because whatever is acquired from outside can be lost. If it manifests from within, then it is not dependent upon causes and conditions that are present in the environment. Therefore, one is able to participate in life and whatever is happening, because there is no longer any threat. They have overcome the fear of being overwhelmed by circumstances and that not being right is a terrible thing. There is an ongoing willingness to learn, and learn from being proven wrong, or even from being chastised, or admonished, and so on. Therefore all experiences become a learning process and consequently we develop more and more.

When one starts to accept oneself in that way, then one is overcoming egocentricity. Egocentricity is overcome when one is fully confident. As long as one is not fully confident, one is always being afflicted by egocentric predicaments, because one sees threats everywhere, they are in a paranoid condition continuously. Right, left, and center, everything becomes a symbolic gesture of a particular threat to oneself. When one begins to become confident, then one is able to see basic goodness all around and in other people, because one is open and unthreatened, one is much more open than one would normally be.

That is the end result of Dzogchen, the actualization of the basis or ground, of essence, nature, and energy. One has become a fully-fledged person who has completely authenticated body, speech, and mind, and is able to realize oneself as the embodiment of the three kayas, or three modes of being of an enlightened person—nirmanakaya, sambhogakaya, and dharmakaya. Once that is achieved, one is able to remain in a state of non-meditation, there is no longer a distinction between a meditative state and a non-meditative state. The meditative experience is a continuous twenty-four hour occurrence.

Notes

Introduction

Ref: *Dzogchen and Mahamudra*, a series of teachings given by Dzogchen Ponlop Rinpoche in 1995 at E-Vam Institute in Melbourne, Australia.

Chapter One
Religion, Spirituality, and Self-knowledge

1. Pavlovian dog—classical conditioning first articulated and tested by Pavlov seeking to condition a dog's behavior. A process commonly used and understood in western psychology referencing the process of pairing neutral stimuli with conditioned stimuli repeatedly to moderate behavior or control behavior. Ref: Psychology, fifth edition, Lester A. Lefton, Allym and Bacon, USA, 1994.

Chapter Two
The Nine Yana System

2. The Mahayana Uttaratantra is the root text of Arya Maitreya, written down by the noble Asanga, founder of the Yogacara school of Mahayana Buddhism. It provides a commentary on the Tathagatagarbha sutras that explains buddha-nature, which the Buddha expounded during his third turning of the Wheel of Dharma. Ref: *Buddha Nature: The Mahayana Uttaratantra Shastra with commentary*, Khenpo Tsultrim Gyamtso Rinpoche & Rosemarie Fuchs, Snow Lion Publications, USA, 2000.

3. The Vedas are a large body of religious texts originating in ancient India. Composed in Vedic Sanskrit, the texts constitute the oldest layer of Sanskrit literature and the oldest scriptures

of Hinduism. Veda means knowledge. There are four Vedas: the Rigveda, the Yajurveda, the Samaveda, and the Atharvaveda. Each Veda has four subdivisions—the Samhitas —mantras and benedictions, the Aranyakas—text on rituals, ceremonies etc, the Brahmanas, and the Upanishads—texts discussing meditation, philosophy and spiritual knowledge. Vedas are *śruti* ("what is heard"), distinguishing them from other religious texts, which are called smṛti ("what is remembered").

Ancient History Encyclopedia. Sanujit Ghose, 2011; https://en.wikipedia.org/wiki/Vedas.

4. Nagarjuna, (150—250 CE) was the founder of the Madhyamaka school of Mahayana Bueddhism. Ref: *Essence of Buddhism: An Introduction to its Philosophy and Practice*, Traleg Kyabgon, Shambhala Publications. USA, 2001.

5. Asanga (4th Century C.E.) was the founder of the Yogacara school of Mahayana Buddhism. Ref: *The Influence of Yogacara on Mahamudra*, Traleg Kyabgon, KTD Publications, USA.

6. The author made a distinction regarding the purpose of the four noble truths and how it is sometimes explained or translated. "The Buddha said that if we want to overcome dissatisfaction, which is intimately linked with our experience of suffering, then we have to deal with craving, grasping, clinging, and attachment—all these exaggerated forms of desire. Now, some people think that Buddhists encourage the idea of eradicating desire altogether, but that is not what the Buddha said. He said that we should try to overcome excessive and exaggerated forms of desire, which manifest as craving, grasping, and so on, because they make our condition worse by increasing our sense of dissatisfaction and discontentment." *Essence of Buddhism: An Introduction to its Philosophy and*

Practice, Traleg Kyabgon, Shambhala Publications. USA, 2001; *Desire: Why it Matters*, Traleg Kyabgon, Shogam Publications, Australia 2019.

7. In contrast to the Sravaka's view of nirvana seen as almost a state of extinction, the Mahayana vision often referred to as "non-abiding nirvana" indicates the importance of not dwelling either in the samsaric condition or in the peaceful bliss of nirvana. It avoids the two extremes of being either immersed in the preoccupation of the samsaric world or to be totally removed from the world. *Essence of Buddhism: An Introduction to its Philosophy and Practice*, Traleg Kyabgon, Shambhala Publications. USA, 2001

8. *Vajrapani, Avalokiteshvara*, and *Manjushri* are iconographically depicted as Buddha's three protectors. They symbolize Buddha's enlightened characteristics of protecting the purity of the Dharma, compassion and wisdom. Vajrapani is one of the earliest bodhisattvas who protects the Buddha and symbolizes the Buddha's power; Avalokiteshvara (Skt.) also commonly known as Chenrezig represents the embodiment of love and compassion. Manjushri represents transcendental wisdom and is associated with learning and music. *Meeting the Buddhas: a Guide to Buddhas, Bodhisattvas, and Tantric Deities*, Windhorse Publications, UK, 1993.

9. Sautantrikas or Sutravadin school (Skt. Suttavāda) is an early school of Buddhism. They relied upon the sutras, canonical scriptures of the Buddha's teachings exclusively. Further commentarial teachings as could be found in the Abhidharma were not seen as containing such authority. They are generally considered to have been a school that was parented by the early Sarvāstivādins' Buddhist school.

10. Arahathood is achieved when the practitioner achieves

nirvana, but is not fully enlightened.

11. Bodhicharyavatara, a famous series of verses written by Shantideva. In English the verses are commonly know as "The Way of the Bodhisattva", or "A Guide to the Bodhisattvas Way of Life." Shantideva (8th Century) was a monk who studied at Nalanda Monastic University.

Chapter Three
Consciousness and Wisdom in Yogacara and Dzogchen

12. The Yogacara school (yoga meaning meditation and cara meaning practice), also know as Chittamantra, is a main school within Mahayana philosophy. Madhyamaka is the other main school. The Yogacarans emphasise the primacy of meditation in understanding ultimate reality. *Essence of Buddhism: An Introduction to its Philosophy and Practice*, Traleg Kyabgon, Shambhala Publications. USA, 2001.

13. Georg Wilhelm Friedrich Hegel (1770-1831). Hegelianism philosophy "the rational alone is real," which means that all reality is capable of being expressed in rational categories. His goal was to reduce reality to a more synthetic unity within the system of absolute idealism.

Chapter Four
Self-Existing Wisdom

14. Nagarjuna says: "The origination of inherent existence from causes is illogical since if inherent existence originates from causes and conditions, all things would thereby become continent." Pratityasamutpada, the interdependence of all things. *Essence of Buddhism: An Introduction to its Philosophy and Practice*, Traleg Kyabgon, Shambhala Publications. USA, 2001.

Chapter Five
Self-Liberation and how Confusion Arises

15. In this context depression and elation refer to the peaks and troughs we often create when relating to ourselves and others. It is not referencing clinical depression as such. Rather it is referencing the samsaric tendency of being emotionally responsive through negative or positive assessment of what we experience as arises in our minds.

16. vinaya sutras set out in great detail the Buddhist monastic rules.

17. Saraha (8th century) is considered to be one of the founders of Buddhist Vajrayana, and in particular the Mahamudra tradition practiced predominantly in the Kagyü school of Tibetan Buddhism, and is commonly considered the highest yoga tantra in that tradition.

18. A mahasiddha is an individual who through sādhanā practice attains the realization of siddhis, psychic and spiritual abilities and powers, and in particular the full realization of their authentic condition, or nature of mind.

Chapter Seven
The Four Yogas, and Meditation and Mental Clarity

19. The four yogas are usually associated with Mahamudra, but Traleg Rinpoche has chosen to use them here in the context of Dzogchen. In Dzogchen the four stages of development are: 1. recognizing rigpa, which is sometimes called manifest dharmata; 2. increased meditative experience; 3. awareness reaching fullness; 4. exhaustion of all concepts and dualistic phenomena.

20. See note 16 for what is mainly meant by depression in this context. For anyone on medications for depression, or under

the supervision of a mental health professional it is advisable to seek guidance before embarking on any meditation practices.

21. Tummo is a Vajrayana practice, one of the six yogas of Naropa. *Vajrayana: An Essential Guide to Practice*, Traleg Kyabgon, Shogam Publications, Australia, 2020.

22. Mahamudra is the highest meditation training of the Sarma or new schools of Tibetan Buddhism, and a special feature of the Kagyü lineage. Further Reading: *Moonbeams of Mahamudra, The Classic Mediation Manual*, Traleg Kyabgon, Shogam Publications, Australia, 2015; Wild awakening: The heart of Mahamudra and Dzogchen, Dzogchen Ponlop, Shambhala, USA, 2003.

23. Vajrayogini is a female diety depicted in semi-wrathful and wrathful forms, or in union with Chakrasamvara, et cetera. Vajrayogini practices predominate in the Kagyü tradition, but are also practiced in all the major schools. *Vajrayogini: Her Visualizations, Rituals, and Forms*, Elizabeth English, Wisdom Publications, USA, 2002.

Chapter Nine
Transcending Self-Image, and the Authentication
of Body, Speech, and Mind

24. Heruka is a category of wrathful deities within Vajrayana. The Yidam denotes the union of bliss and the emptiness of all phenomena.

25. The ghost in the machine means the consciousness or mind carried in a physical entity. Gilbert Ryle coined the term in his 1949 work The Concept of Mind as a criticism of René Descartes. Descartes believed in dualism, the idea that the human mind is not physical, that it exists independently of the human brain.

26. Ensure you check with your doctor or health care professional before attempting any physical exercises.

27. Martin Buber (1878–1965) philosopher is known for his philosophy of dialogue, a form of existentialism centered on the distinction between the I–Thou relationship and the I–It relationship.

Glossary

Key: (skt) Sanskrit; (tib) Tibetan phonetics; (*Wylie*) Standard Tibetan phonetic protocols as per the Wylie system. Whenever possible the Tibetan phonetics are followed by the Wylie spelling, in which case normally only "(*Wylie*)" is used to indicate the two version or shared spelling of the Tibetan phonetics. There are a few exceptions.

alankara (skt) Abhisamayalamkara (skt) མངོན་པར་རྟོགས་པའི་རྒྱན། Ngon par tog pa'i gen (tib), *Mngon par rtogs pa'i rgyan (Wylie)*. Maitreya's "*Ornament for Clear Realization.*" As the Mahayana sutra alankara says: "seven factors that distinguish the Mahayana from the Hinayana."

alayavijnana (skt) ཀུན་གཞི་རྣམ་ཤེས། kun zhi nam she (tib) *kun gzhi rnam shes (Wylie)*. The eighth level is the unconscious which can be translated as "sub-stratum of awareness," "fundamental consciousness," or "storehouse consciousness."

Anuyoga or Anuttarayoga(skt), རྣལ་འབྱོར་བླ་མེད་རྒྱུད། Naljor lamed gyud (tib), *rnal'byor bla med rgyud (Wylie)*.

Avoloketisvara or Padmapani (skt) སྤྱན་རས་གཟིགས། ཡང་ན། ཕྱག་ན་པདྨོ Chanre zig (tib), *Spyan ras gzigs (Wylie)* or Chagna Pemo, *Phyag na padmo (Wylie)*. A bodhisattva who embodies the compassion of all Buddhas. This bodhisattva is variably depicted, described and portrayed in different cultures as either male or female. Known as Chenrezig, and Avalokiteśvara. In Chinese Buddhism Avalokiteśvara has evolved into the somewhat different female figure Guanyin, also known in Japan as Kanzeon or Kannon.

bhagadvadgita The *Bhagavad Gita* "The Song of God" ལེགས་ལྡན་ནག་པོའི་གླུ། leg dan nag po'i lu, *legs ldan nag po'i glu (Wylie)*, often referred to as the Gita, is a 700c verse Sanskrit scripture that is part of the Hindu epic *Mahabharata* which it is a part, is attributed to sage Vyasa whose full name was *Krishna Dvaipayana*, also called *Veda Vyasa*. The great modern Tibetan scholar Late Gedun Chosphel had translated Chapter 10th, 11th and 12th into Tibetan.

blo burwa'i dri ma (tib) སློ་བུར་བའི་དྲི་མ། "adventitious defilements." Recognition that all adventitious obstacles need to be removed.

Bodhicharyavatara, Jang chub sempa'i chod pa la jugpa བྱང་ཆུབ་སེམས་དཔའི་སྤྱོད་པ་ལ་འཇུག་པ། *byang chub sems dpa'i spyod pa la 'jug pa. (Wylie)*. Common English translation is known as *"A guide to the Boddhisattav's way of life."*

bodhichitta(skt) བྱང་ཆུབ་ཀྱི་སེམས། jangchub ki sem, *byang chub kyi sems (Wylie)*. The englightened mind.

chos ཆོས། dharma(skt), religion.

cig carwa གཅིག་ཅར་བ། *gcig car wa (Wylie)* and rimcan pa རིམ་ཅན་པ། rim can pa (Wylie). In Dzogchen the approach is instantaneous, sudden, gcig car wa, as opposed to gradual, Rim can pa (tib).

dag nang དག་སྣང་། *dag snang (Wylie)*. Pure vision or pure visualization. The concept of dag snang can be translated as "presence of numen," "sacred outlook," or "purity perception."

de tong བདེ་སྟོང་། *Bde stong (Wylie)*. The first type of non-conceptuality is known as "non-conceptuality of bliss and emptiness."

dharma ཆོས། chos and dhatu (skt) དབྱིངས། ying, *dbyings (Wylie)*. The word for space is དབྱིངས། dbyings (Wylie), dhātu in Sanskrit. The word "space" can be used because the dharmadhatu is like the body or realm of empty space where different things, like clouds, birds, and airplanes can fly around without obstruction. This is because the nature of space is empty. dharmas (skt) ཆོས། cos—phenomena, attributes. In this particular case dharmas means "entities or attribute."

dharmadhatu (skt) ཆོས་ཀྱི་དབྱིངས། Cho ski ying, *Chos kyi dbyings* (*Wylie*). The nature of phenomena, or the primordial wisdom cognizing the reality of phenomena.

dharmakaya(skt) ཆོས་སྐུ། chos ku, *chos sku* (*Wylie*). The truth body. The foundation of all qualities, the source of the four kayas. See also Kaya.

Dhyani Buddhas རྒྱལ་བ་རིགས་ལྔ། Gyalwa rig nga, *rGyalwa rigs lnga* (*Wylie*). The five Dhyani Buddhas are celestial Buddhas who are included in visualization practices. The word Dhyani is derived from the Sanskrit dhyana, meaning "meditation." The Dhyani Buddhas are also called Jinas ("Victors" or "Conquerors"). In tantric practices the Dhyani Buddhas transmute the five poisons into their transcendent wisdoms. The Tibetan Book of the Dead recommends that the devotee meditate on the Dhyani Buddhas to help the five wisdoms to arise to replace personal negative forces. The five dhayani Buddhas Panca jina (skt), རྒྱལ་བ་རིགས་ལྔ།། gyalwa rig nga, *Rgyalwa rigs lnga* (*Wylie*).

1. Vairocana(skt) རྣམ་པར་སྣང་མཛད། Nampar nang zed, *Rnam par snang mdzad* (*Wylie*).

2. Aksobhya(skt) མི་སྐྱོད་པ། Mi kyodpa, *Mi-skyodpa* (*Wylie*).

3. Ratnasambhava(skt). རིན་ཆེན་འབྱུང་གནས། Rinchen Jungnes, *Rinchen 'byung gnas* (*Wylie*).

4. Amitabha(skt) འོད་དཔག་མེད། Wod pag med, *Wod drag med* (*Wylie*).

5. Amoghasiddhi(skt) དོན་ཡོད་གྲུབ་པ། Donyoe drub pa, *Dhonyod grubpa* (*Wylie*).

don དོན། artha(skt). Meaning. The fourth one is Don in Tibetan, which means "meaning."

dondam den pa དོན་དམ་བདེན་པ། *dondam bdenpa* (*Wylie*), paramartha satya (skt), the ultimate truth. གུན་རྫོབ་བདེན་པ། kunzob denpa, *kun rdzob bden pa* (*Wylie*). samvrti satya (skt), conventional truth. དབྱེར་མེད། yermed, *dbyer med* (*Wylie*), abhinna (skt) means "The inseparable". The outlook of the practitioner of maha yoga is to keep three things in mind དོན་དམ། dondam, གུན་རྫོབ། kunzob, *kunrdzob* (*Wylie*), and དབྱེར་མེད། dbyer med in Tibetan. *Dondam bden pa* means "Absolute or Ultimate truth," *kun rdzob bden pa* (*Wylie*), means "Conventional or Relative truth", and *dbyer med* means "undivided or inseparable" or "non-divisibility" of the two.

drib སྒྲིབ། *sgirb* (*Wylie*), means obstructions or obscurations. All the mental imbalances, neurosis, psychosis, are called *sgrib*.

dribpa nyis སྒྲིབ་པ་གཉིས། *sgrib pa gnyis* (*Wylie*). Two Obstructions:

1. Klesavarana (skt) ཉོན་མོངས་པའི་སྒྲིབ་པ། Nyon mong pa'i dribbpa, *Nyon mongs pa'i sgrib pa* (*Wylie*), delusive obscuration to liberation.

2. Jnanavarana (skt) ཤེས་བྱའི་སྒྲིབ་པ། shes jai dribpa, *Shes bya'i sgrib pa* (*Wylie*), obstructions to omniscience.

drol lug chen po nga གྲོལ་ལུགས་ཆེན་པོ་བཞི་ལྔ། *grol lugs chen po bzhi lnga* (*Wylie*). Five kinds of great releases or liberations.

1. Ye drol ཡེ་གྲོལ། *Ye grol* (*Wylie*). The first meaning that the individual has been freed right from the beginning.

2. Rang drol རང་གྲོལ། *Rang grol* (*Wylie*). The second meaning self-liberation.

3. Cer drol གཅེར་གྲོལ། *Gcer grol* (*Wylie*). The third, Gcer means naked, and *grol* means to become liberated again.

4. Tha drol མཐའ་གྲོལ། *Mtha' grol* (*Wylie*). The fourth means that one is liberated because one is no longer confined by labels and extreme views.

5. Cig drol གཅིག་གྲོལ། *Gcig grol* (*Wylie*). The fifth one is the most important in this particular system. *Gcig grol* means "liberation

of one," this particular point refers to *rigpa*, basic awareness.

drug de དྲུག་སྡེ། *drug sde* (*Wylie*). Sad vargika (skt), the six close disciples of Buddha Sakyamuni who were punished by Buddha for breaching their disciplines.

1. དགའ་བོ། gawo, *dga'wo* (*Wylie*), Nanda (skt).
2. ཉེ་དགའ་བོ། Nyega wo, *Nye dga' wo* (*Wylie*). Upananda(skt).
3. འགྲོ་མགྱོགས། dro gyog, *'Gro mgyogs* (*Wylie*), Asvaka(skt).
4. ནབས་སོ། Nabso, *Nabs so* (*Wylie*), Punarvasu(skt).
5. འདུན་པ། Dunpa, *'Dun pa* (*Wylie*), Chanda(skt).
6. འཆར་ཀ། *'Char ka* (*Wylie*), Udayi(skt).

gnas གནས། gyu གྱུ། rigs རིགས། ying དབྱིངས། In order to prepare oneself to approach Dzogchen meditation there are four things one must understand. The first three are *gnas, gyu, rigs*, and the fourth one is *ying* in Tibetan. gnas gyu rigs gsum, གནས། གྱུ། རིགས་དང་གསུམ། *Rigs* is bare awareness. Usually, in the Dzogchen vocabulary or terminology, it is called gnas gyu rigs gsum, pang lang, སྤང་བླང་། *spangs, blang* (*Wylie*). As has been said in the Dzogchen texts, one should not engage in either *spangs* or *blangs. Spangs* སྤང་སི། means to discard, *blangs* བླང་སི། means to cultivate.

gyu གྱུ། see gnas གནས།.

gzhi གཞི། fundamental or root. Lam ལམ། path and dras bu འབྲས་བུ། *bras bu* (*Wylie*), fruit or result. They have their own starting point, own idea of the path, and own idea of the goal.

Heruka བདེ་མཆོག ། de chog, *bde mchog* (*Wylie*), or འཁོར་ལོ་བདེ་མཆོག khorlo dechog, *'khor lo bde mchog* (*Wylie*). A tantric deity belonging to the mother tantra of the highest class of Tantra.

jing བྱིང་། *Bying* (*Wylie*). Laya (skt). Losing heart, lethargy and laxity. All our experiences, in some way or other, that lead us away from mental clarity or meditation comes under two categories—that of depression, *bying*, and elation, *rgod* རྒོད་, Uddhatya (skt.), it also means mental agitation or excitement.

Jñanasattva (skt.); Tib. ཡེ་ཤེས་སེམས་དཔའ། Yeshe sempa, *Yeshes sems dpa'* (*Wylie*), "wisdom being:"

1. The actual wisdom deities you invite to come and bless the deities of the mandala you are visualizing.

2. It refers to the deity visualized in the heart centre of the samayasattva.

jod ja, བརྗོད་བྱ། *brjod bya* (*Wylie*), abhidhaya (skt) meaning subject matter; object of expression, and also referred to as "the subject of discourse."

ka, བཀའ། *bka'* (*Wylie*), Vacana or Buddhavacana (skt). The word of the Buddha, direct teachings of the Buddha.

Ka dag ཀ་དག Primordial purity.

karma ལས། *Las* (*Wylie*), Law of causality. Karma is divided into various types.

karmic ལས་འབྲས། Las dras, *Las'bras* (*Wylie*), karma-phala(skt), karmic tendencies, law of causality.

kayas, five: Kayas སྐུ། Various aspects or states of buddhahood. Categorized into two, three, four, and five kata groupings:

two kayas: dharmakaya ཆོས་སྐུ། chos ku, *chos sku* (*Wylie*), the absolute body, and rupakaya གཟུགས་སྐུ། *gzugs sku* (*Wylie*), the body of form.

three kayas:

1. the dharmakaya, ཆོས་སྐུ། chos ku, *chos sku* (*Wylie*), or absolute body;

2. the sambhogakaya, ལོང་སྐུ། long ku, *long sku* (*Wylie*), or body of divine enjoyment;

3. the nirmanakaya, སྤྲུལ་སྐུ། tulku, *sprul sku* (*Wylie*), or manifested body. These correspond to the mind, speech, and body

respectively of an enlightened buddha.

four kayas: the svabhavikakaya, དེ་བོ་ཉིད་སྐུ། ngo wo nyid ku, *ngo wo nyid sku* (*Wylie*), or essential body, is to be added to the three kayas and represents their inseparability (dbyer med).

five kayas: to the three kayas one adds the avikaravajrakaya, མི་འགྱུར་རྡོ་རྗེའི་སྐུ། migyur dorje ku, *mi'gyur dor rje'i sku* (*Wylie*), the "unchanging vajra body," and the abhisambodhikaya, མངོན་པར་བྱང་ཆུབ་པའི་སྐུ། ngon par jangchupa'i ku, *mngon par gyang chub pa'i sku* (*Wylie*), "body of total enlightenment." Vajrakaya of the unchanging natural state is the embodiment of the enlightened activity of all the buddhas and the perfect kaya of complete awakening is the embodiment of all the buddhas' enlightened qualities. *Rangjung Yeshe Wiki, Dharma Dictionary. Rigpa Wiki.*

khor gsum mi rtog pa འཁོར་གསུམ་མི་རྟོག་པ། 'Khor gsum mi rtog pa (*Wylie*), the lack of conceptual imagination of the three circles. The wisdom that is free of any conceptual recognition of the three— agent, activity, and goal—as having any inherent identity of their own, knowing these as being empty or free of inherent existence. This means one no longer makes distinction between the subject who is practicing the virtue, the act of the practice the virtue, and the person who is the object of virtue.

kriya, charya, and yoga བྱ་རྒྱུད། Jagyud, *bya rgyud* (*Wylie*); སྤྱོད་རྒྱུད། Chod gyud, Spyod rgyud (*Wylie*); རྣལ་འབྱོར་རྒྱུད། Naljor gyud, *Rnal 'byor rgyud* (*Wylie*). The first three yanas related with Tantra are kriya, charya, and yoga, the so called "outer tantras."

ku སྐུ། *sku* (*Wylie*), kaya (skt). Exalted body, the body becomes what is known as sku (Wylie), whereas the ordinary body is known as ལུས། *lus* (*Wylie*). *Also see Kaya.*

sku-nga སྐུ་ལྔ། *sku lnga* (*Wylie*). Panca-kaya (Skt), Five Kayas. *Also see Kaya.*

kun zhi ཀུན་གཞི། *kun gzhi* (*Wylie*). The fourth level of consciousness in the Dzogchen system often translated as the the sub-stratum.

kun zhi gyalpo ཀུན་གཞི་རྒྱལ་པོ། *kungzhi rgyalpo* (*Wylie*), "king of self-creation."

kyerim བསྐྱེད་རིམ། *bskyed rim* (*Wylie*), utpattikrama(skt.), the generation or development stage practice.

lam rim ལམ་རིམ། the "graded path to enlightenment."

lhundrub ལྷུན་འགྲུབ། *lhun'grub* (*Wylie*). Anabhoga/nirabhoga (skt). *Spontaneously establishment.*

lo burwai dry ma བློ་བུར་བའི་དྲི་མ། *blo burwa'i drama* (*Wylie*), Agantuka-mala(Skt) "adventitious defilements." Meaning, when all adventitious obstacles are removed.

lung ལུང་། upadesa(skt) oral transmission, precept or spiritual instruction.

mahamudra ཕྱག་རྒྱ་ཆེན་པོ། chag gya chenpo, *phyag rgya chenpo* (*Wylie*). "The Great Seal."

maha-sukha བདེ་བ་ཆེན་པོ། deva chenpo, *bdewa chen po* (*Wylie*). Great bliss, great happiness.

Mahayana ཐེག་ཆེན་གྱི་ཆེན་པོ་བདུན། *Theg chen gyi chenpo bdun* (*Wylie*), Seven Greatnenesses of the Mahayana. *Dung kar's Tibetan Encyclopedic Dictionary.*

1. Migpa chenpo, *Dmigs pa chen po* (*Wylie*) དམིགས་པ་ཆེན་པོ། The first factor that distinguishes the Mahayana from the Hinayana is called *dmigs pa* in Tibetan. dmigs pa means "the vision."

2. Dunpa chenpo, *Sgrub pa chen po* (*Wylie*) སྒྲུབ་པ་ཆེན་པོ། The second factor is *Sgrub pa* in Tibetan. *Sgrub pa* means "aspirations."

3. Yeshes chenpo, *Yeshes chen po* (*Wylie*) ཡེ་ཤེས་ཆེན་པོ། The third one is yeshes in Tibetan, which means "wisdom."

4. Tsondus chenpo, *brtson, 'grus chen po* (*Wylie*) བརྩོན་འགྲུས་ཆེན་པོ། The fourth one is *brtson 'grus* meaning "great effort."

5. Thab la khas pa, *Thabs la mkhas pa chen po* (*Wylie*) ཐབས་ལ་མཁས་པ་ཆེན་པོ། The fifth one is *Thabs la mkhas pa* which means "skilful means."

6. Yang dag drubpa, *Yang dag sgrub pa* (*Wylie*) ཡང་དག་སྒྲུབ་པ་ཆེན་པོ། The sixth factor refers to becoming endowed with the greater powers of the Buddha.

7. Thrinlas, *'Phrin las* (*Wylie*) འཕྲིན་ལས་ཆེན་པོ། The seventh refers to becoming a Buddha. The bodhisattva is able to engage in unceasing Buddha activity for the benefit of others.

mandala (skt) མཎྜལ། a divine mansion or an offering to one's spiritual master, in which one visualizes offering the entire universe and its precious contents et cetera.

Manjusri (skt) འཇམ་དཔལ་དབྱངས། Jampal yang, *Jam dpal dbyangs* (*Wylie*), is a Bodhisattva who embodies the wisdom energy of all the Buddhas. Manjusri is frequently found in various sutras, such as the Heart Sutra.

manovijnana (skt) ཡིད། *yid* (Wylie). The seventh level of consciousness often translated as "egocentric mentation."

Maudgaliputra or Maudgalyayanaputra མོའུ་འགལ་གྱི་བུ། Mogal gi bu, Mo-wu 'gal gyi bu (Wylie), was one of the Sakyamuni Buddha's closest disciples. A contemporary of such disciples as Subhuti, Śāriputra, and Mahākasyapa. He is considered the second of the Buddha's two foremost disciples (foremost in psychic powers), together with Śāriputra.

nalmar naspa མནལ་མར་གནས་པ། *mnal mar gnaspa* (*Wylie*). Is a Dzogchen technical term. *Mnal mar* means "state of naturalness," *gnaspa* means "exist." So the full meaning is existing in the state of naturalness.

nam min རྣམ་སྨིན། rnam smin (Wylie), vipaka/prapaka (skt). Fruition or maturation, referencing a karma result or reward.

nang wa སྣང་བ། snang wa (Wylie) and ཡུལ། yul (Wylie). *Snang wa* means appearance or visions, and *Yul* means the object one perceives. That is referring to the whole phenomenal experience. What we immediately perceive is constructed by the mind, but the object of appearance, *Yul* is not created by the mind.

nyam ཉམས། nyams (Wylie), hana/hiyate(skt), means a feeling, experience, or vision. *Nyams* can also be translated as "experiential attunement."

nyug mar གཉུག་མར་གནས་པ། gnyug mar (Wylie). Nyug ma means innermost, intrinsic; fundamental unmistaken nature.

Paramitas, six Sad paramitas(skt) ཕར་ཕྱིན་དྲུག Phar-phyin drug (Wylie). Six Perfections.

1. Dana paramita(skt) སྦྱིན་པའི་ཕར་ཕྱིན། jinpa'i phar chin, *sbyin pa'i phar phyin* (Wylie). The perfection of generosity, giving.

2. Shila paramita(skt) ཚུལ་ཁྲིམས་ཀྱི་ཕར་ཕྱིན། Tsultrim ki pharchin, *Tshulthrim kyi phar phyin* (Wylie). Perfection of morality.

3. Ksanti paramita(skt) བཟོད་པའི་ཕར་ཕྱིན། Zodpa'I pharchin, *Bzod pa'i phar phyin* (Wylie). Perfection of patience.

4. Virya paramita(skt) བརྩོན་འགྲུས་ཀྱི་ཕར་ཕྱིན། Tsondrus ki pharchin, *Brtson drus kyi phar phyin* (Wylie). Perfection of efforts.

5. Dhyana paramita(skt) བསམ་གཏན་གྱི་ཕར་ཕྱིན། Samten ji pharchin, *Gsam gtan gyi phar phyin* (Wylie). Perfection of concentration.

6. Prajna paramita(skt) ཤེས་རབ་ཀྱི་ཕར་ཕྱིན། Sherab ki pharchin, *Shesrab kyi phar phyin* (Wylie). Perfection of wisdom.

parinispanna (skt) ཡོངས་གྲུབ། yong drub, *yongs grub* (Wylie). The first order of reality is "the ground of being," or "ideally absolute."

paratantra (skt) གཞན་དབང་། zhan wang, *gzhan dbang* (Wylie). The second order of reality is called "causal relationship," or "relative."

parikalpita (skt) གུན་རྟགས། kun tag, *kun rtags* (*Wylie*). The third order of reality is "conceptual apparatus," or "notional-conceptual."

prana སྲོག sog, *srog* (*Wylie*), life-force. According to vinaya and the Abhidharma tradition it is the vital energy that acts as the basis for consciousness and the warmth of a being. Prana literally means "breath."

pratityasamutpada རྟེན་ཅིང་འབྲེལ་བར་འབྱུང་བ། ten cing drelwar jung wa, *Rten cing 'bral bar 'byung ba* (*Wylie*), interdependent origination; dependant co-origination. In general, the twelve links of interdependent origination in its highest sense of understanding explains phenomena being dependant on each other and hence is lacking inherent existence.

rang jung yeshe རང་འབྱུང་ཡེ་ཤེས། *rang 'byung yeshes* (*Wylie*), "self-existing wisdom."

rigpa རིག་པ། *rigpa* (*Wylie*), a certain state of awareness in Dzogchen.

sadhana(skt) སྒྲུབ་ཐབས། drub thab, *sgrub thabs* (*Wylie*), meaning "a means of accomplishing," through the sadhana practices.

sal tong གསལ་སྟོང་། gsal stong (Wylie). The second one is called the "non-conceptuality of clarity and emptiness." The third aspect is known as "non-conceptuality of reality," which is non-conceptuality of Ying དབྱིངས། dbying (Wylie), or field.

sal tong གསལ་སྟོང་། *gsal stong* (*Wylie*). The second aspect of "non-conceptuality of clarity and emptiness." The third aspect is known as "non-conceptuality of reality," which is non-conceptuality of Ying དབྱིངས། *dbying* (*Wylie*), or field, sal tong zung jug གསལ་སྟོང་ཟུང་འཇུག | *gsal stong zung 'jug* (*Wylie*), the non-duality, or unity, of luminosity and emptiness. De tong zung jug བདེ་སྟོང་ཟུང་འཇུག *bde stong zung 'jug* (*Wylie*), the unity, or inseparability, of bliss and emptiness. Rig tong zung jug རིག་སྟོང་ཟུང་འཇུག *rig stong zung 'jug* (*Wylie*), the inseparability of bare awareness and emptiness, nang tong zung jug སྣང་སྟོང་ཟུང་འཇུག *snang stong zung 'jug* (*Wylie*), the inseparability of appearance, or phenomena, and emptiness.

Samayasattva (Skt) དམ་ཚིག་སེམས་དཔའ། Dam tsig sempa, *Dam tshig sems dpa'* (*Wylie*). In terms of the "generation" or "development phase" of practice, the goal is to purify our perception into the purity of our inherent nature *samayasattva* or commitment being. This arises in the form of the deity, having first practised the three samadhis.

samsara(skt) འཁོར་བ། *'khor wa* (*Wylie*), cyclic existence, becoming caught in "cyclic existence."

sang chod གསང་སྤྱོད། *gsang spyod* (*Wylie*). Three types of action. The first is gsang spyod or "secret action." Rigpa tulshug རིག་པ་རྩལ་ཞུགས། *rigpa rtulzhugs* (*Wylie*), is the second meaning "actualization of rigpa." Tsog chod ཚོགས་སྤྱོད། *tshogs spyod* (*Wylie*), the third is known as "communal participation."

sem nyid སེམས་ཉིད། *sems nyid* (*Wylie*), cittatva (skt), mind in itself.

shamatha ཞི་གནས། Zhi-nas, *Gzhi gnas* (*Wylie*), calm abiding meditation.

Shariputra (skt), or Sāriputta (Pāli) ཤ་རིའི་བུ། Shari bu, *Sha r'i bu* (*Wylie*), a master of Wisdom. In the Heart Sutra, the bodhisattva Avalokiteśvara preaches to Shariputra. Maudgalyayana and Śāriputra were once disciples of Sañjaya Belaṭṭhaputta, the skeptic, but they both later became two chief disciples of the Buddha.

shastra (skt) བསྟན་བཅོས། tan chos, *bstan bcos* (*Wylie*), treatise, commentaries based on Buddha's direct teachings (bka'gyur) by Indian panditas or acharyas.

Sravaka's, four main traditional schools. ཉན་ཐོས་ཀྱི་རྩ་བའི་སྡེ་པ་བཞི། *Nyan thos kyi rtsa wa'i sde pa bzhi* (*Wylie*), Catvari mula Sravaka nikayah (Skt).

1. Mulasarvastivadin (skt), བམས་ཅད་ཡོད་པར་སྨྲ་བའི་སྡེ། *Thams cad yodpar smra wa'i sde (Wylie)*;
2. Mahasamghika (skt), ཕལ་ཆེན་པའི་སྡེ་པ། *Phal chen pa'i sde (Wylie)*;
3. Sthavira (skt) གནས་བརྟན་པའི་སྡེ་པ། *Gnas brtan pa'i sde pa (Wylie)*;
4. Sammitya (skt) མང་པོས་བཀུར་བའི་སྡེ། *Mang pos bkur wa'i sde (Wylie)*.

Sravaka's two schools ཉན་ཐོས་ཀྱི་སྡེ་གཉིས། *Nyan thos kyi sde gnyis (Wylie)*.

1. བྱེ་བྲག་སྨྲ་བ། jed drag mawa, Bye brag smra wa (Wylie), Vaibhasika (skt).
2. མདོ་སྡེ་པ། dho depa, mdo sde pa (Wylie), Sautantrika (skt).

Subhūti (skt) རབ་འབྱོར། Rabjor, *Rab'byor (Wylie)*. Born in Sravasti མཉན་ཡོད། (Mnyan-yod), India. The disciple foremost of those living remote and in peace (*araṇavihārīnamaggo*), and of those who were worthy of gifts (*dakkhiṇeyyānaṃ*). He appears in several sutras of Mahāyāna Buddhism which teach Śūnyatā (Emptiness). He is the subject of the Subhūti Sutta. In the lineage of the Panchen Lamas of Tibet there were considered to be four "Indian" and three Tibetan incarnations of Amitabha Buddha before Khedrup Gelek Pelzang, recognised as the first Panchen Lama. The Panchan Lama's lineage starts with Subhuti.

sunyata (skt) སྟོང་པ་ཉིད། tongpa nyid, *stong pa nyid* (Wylie), emptiness.

sutra (skt) མདོ། dho, *mdo (Wylie)*, sets of discourses from the in the Buddhist Canon (bka'gyur).

thogpa medpa ཐོགས་པ་མེད་པ། *thogspa medpa (Wylie)*, Apratighati (skt), unobstructed or without obstacles; "devoid of subject and object." When the understanding emerges the person is no longer disposed to or dependent upon a rational understanding of things.

thug je ཐུགས་རྗེ། *thugs rje (Wylie)*, Compassion, or responsiveness.

thugs ཐུགས། the third realization that comes from anuyoga practice.

togpa རྟོགས་པ། *rtogs pa* (*Wylie*). adhigama/abhigamana (skt), meaning, one should seek to realize, cognize, have realisation, and so develop wisdom or insight. If one can do this effectively then one will gain *rtogs pa*. That is, one will understand the workings of the mind.

tripitaka (skt) སྡེ་སྣོད་གསུམ། de nod sum, *sde snod gsum* (*Wylie*), the three baskets of teachings. Buddha's teachings are generally divided into three categories according to their subject matter and trainings as described:

1. འདུལ་བའི་སྡེ་སྣོད། dulwa'i de nod, *'dul wa'i sde snod* (*Wylie*). vinaya pitaka (skt), the basket of teachings on monastic discipline, rules and ethics.

2. མདོ་སྡེའི་སྡེ་སྣོད། do de'i de nod, *mdo sde'i sde snod* (*Wylie*), Sutra pitaka (skt), the basket of teachings in discourses mainly emphasizes the training of concentration.

3. མངོན་པའི་སྡེ་སྣོད། Ngon pa'i de nod, *Mngon pa'i sde snod* (*Wylie*), Abhidharma pitaka (skt). The basket of teachings on knowledge mainly emphasizing the training of wisdom.

tsan ma medpa མཚན་མ་མེད་པ། *mtshen ma medpa* (*Wylie*), alakshana (skt). The inner tantras do not place emphasis on sign so much and are therefore called *mtshanma med pa*, meaning "signless."

tsan nyid. མཚན་ཉིད། *mtshan nyid* (*Wylie*), Laksana (skt), characteristics or mark.

tsen ma མཚན་མ། *mtshan ma* (*Wylie*), Lakshana (skt), meaning either symbol or sign.

tsol med རྩོལ་མེད། It is said that one's action should be effortless.

tummo གཏུམ་མོ། *gtum mo* (*Wylie*), Candali (skt), generating inner heat. Through *gtum mo* practice one can generate inner heat, the practice is known as tummy or mystic heat yoga.

uttaratantra(skt) རྒྱུད་བླ་མ། gyud lama, *rgyud blama* (*Wylie*), (Maitreya's) great vehicle treatise on the sublime continuum.

vajra(skt) རྡོ་རྗེ། dorjee, *rdo rje* (*Wylie*). Diamond hard, a symbol of strength and indestructibility, also a tantric ritual object."Vajra" normally means "indestructibleness."

Vajrapani (skt) ཕྱག་ན་རྡོ་རྗེ། chagna dorjee, *Phyagna rDo rje* (*Wylie*), vajra holder. A bodhisattava who embodies the might and power of all the Buddhas.

Vajrasattva རྡོ་རྗེ་སེམས་དཔའ། dorje sempa, *rdoje sems dpa* (*Wylie*). "The practice of Vajrasattva and recitation of his mantra are particularly effective for purifying negative actions. In the lineage of the Great Perfection he is the Sambhogkaya Buddha." A Tantric Deity dedicated to purification and elimination of unwholesome deeds and appears in both peaceful and wrathful forms.

Vajrayogini Dorjee Naljorma རྡོ་རྗེ་རྣལ་འབྱོར་མ། *Rdo rje rnal 'byor ma* (*Wylie*) Vajrayogini was originally taught by Buddha Vajradhara who manifested in the form of Heruka to expound the Root Tantra of Heruka. It was in this tantra that the Vajrayogini practice was explained. All the many lineages of instructions on Vajrayogini can be traced back to this original revelation. Of these lineages, there are three that are most commonly practiced called as kha chod kor sum: མཁའ་སྤྱོད་སྐོར་གསུམ། *Mkha spyod skor gsum* (*Wylie*). "The three cycles of Khasarpana Dakini."

1. Naro khacho ནཱ་རོ་མཁའ་སྤྱོད། *Naro mkha spyod* (*Wylie*) lineage, which was transmitted from Vajrayogini to Naropa;

2. Maitri-khacho མེ་ཏྲི་མཁའ་སྤྱོད། *Maitri mkha spyod* (*Wylie*) lineage, which was transmitted from Vajrayogini to Maitripa;

3. Indra-khacho ཨིནྡྲ་མཁའ་སྤྱོད། *Indra mkha spyod* (*Wylie*) lineage, which was transmitted from Vajrayogini to Indrabodhi. This commentary to the generation and completion stages of the

Highest Yoga Tantra practice of Vajrayogini is based on the instructions of the Narokhacho lineage.

Vedas, four Catvaraveda (skt) རིག་བྱེད་བཞི། Rig jed zhi, *rigbyed bzhi* (*Wylie*)

1. Rig veda (veda of poetry) ངེས་བརྗོད། *nges jod, nges brjod* (*Wylie*)

2. Yajur veda (veda of sacrifice) མཆོད་སྦྱིན། chod jin, *mchod sbyin* (*Wylie*)

3. Sama veda (veda of aphorisms) སྙན་ཚིག། nyen tsig, *Snyan tshig* (*Wylie*)

4. Atharvaveda (veda of administration) སྲིད་སྲུང། Sid sung, *Srid srung* (*Wylie*)

vikalpa/Samkalpa(skt) རྣམ་རྟོག། nam tog, *rnam rtog* (*Wylie*). By engaging in the practice of Dzogchen, one begins to become dispossessed of all the karmic traces, dispositions, and intellectual perplexity.

vinaya (skt) འདུལ་བ། dulwa, *'dulwa* (*Wylie*), monastic discipline. It was one of the five main divisions of study in the monastic universities of Tibet.

The Five major studies:

1. Pramana (skt) ཚད་མ། tsad ma, *tshad ma* (*Wylie*), valid cognition.

2. Prajna-paramita(skt) ཕར་ཕྱིན། phar chin, *phar phyin* (*Wylie*), perfection of wisdom.

3. Madhayamaka(skt) དབུམ། uma, *dbuma* (*Wylie*).

4. Abhidharma kosa (skt) ཆོས་མངོན་མཛོད། chos ngon pa zod, *chos mngon mdzod* (*Wylie*).

5. Vinaya(skt) འདུལ་བ། dulwa, *'dulwa* (*Wylie*), monastic discipline. See also "tripitaka," and the discussion on the three baskets.

vipashyana (skt) ལྷག་མཐོང། lhag mthong, Penetrative insight meditation, application of analysis on an internal or external object.

yana (skt) ཐེག་པ། thegpa, vehicles or capacity. When practicing the dharma one embarks on the practices and approach systems, literally meaning "vehicles."

yogas, four: The first yoga is called "yoga of one pointedness," tse chik རྩེ་གཅིག Rtse gcig (*Wylie*), ekagra (skt). The second one is called "yoga of non-discrimination," tros-dral སྤྲོས་བྲལ། Spros bral (*Wylie*), aprapanca (skt). The third one is called the "yoga of one flavor," or "yoga of one taste," ro chik རོ་གཅིག Ro gcig (*Wylie*), ekarasa (skt). The fourth one is called the "yoga of non-meditation," gom med སྒོམ་མེད། Sgom med (*Wylie*), abhavana (skt).

yugananda(skt) ཟུང་འཇུག zung 'jug (*Wylie*). Unification, state of union, e.g. the union of calm-abiding and penetrative insight meditation or the union of bliss and emptiness.

zhan sel གཞན་སེལ། gzhan sel (*Wylie*), means something similar to "principle of exclusion."

zhi གཞི། gzhi (*Wylie*), "ground of being."

zhiwa ཞི་བ། shanti(skt), peace. Meaning the person is at peace.

zogpa chenpo, རྫོགས་པ་ཆེན་པོ། Rdzogs pa chen po, rDzogchen (*Wylie*), or Maha Ati, one's existential being. Rdzogs pa chen po is the Tibetan translation of the Sanskrit word Maha Ati, and literally means "the great ultimate," or "the great fulfilment." rdzogs pa means "fulfilment or accomplishment," and chen po means "great".

Zogrim རྫོགས་རིམ། rdzogs rim (Wylie), Sampanna krama (skt). Completion stage or   fulfilment stage.

Index